compleme

MEDICıNE

CAREERS HANDBOOK

Jane Foulkes

ead*way* · Hodder & Stoughton

British Library Cataloguing in Publication Data

Foulkes, Jane MA PGCE
  The Complementary Medicine Careers Handbook
  I. Title
  610.69

  ISBN 0–340–54910–6

First published 1991

Typeset by Serif Tree, Kidlington, Oxon

Printed in Great Britain for Headway, a division of Hodder and Stoughton Ltd,
Mill Road, Dunton Green, Sevenoaks, Kent by Page Bros, Norwich

Contents

Acknowledgements

The author and publisher would like to thank John Walmsley for his kind permission to use the photographs in this book.

The Institute for Complementary Medicine may be contacted at: Unit 4, Tavern Quay, Rope Street, Rotherhithe, London SE16. Please state exactly what sort of information you need and enclose a large stamped addressed envelope.

How To Use
This Book

Starting or changing a career is one of the most important steps in anyone's life history. Some lucky people know from the outset what they want to do, take all the right decisions at the right time and glide straight on to success. Many others lack the necessary information, drift or are pushed in directions that do not suit them and pass unfulfilled lives.

This book should help you make the decisions rather than letting them happen to you. As you read the sections, keep checking. Does the personality description fit you? Does your educational background debar you from the discipline under discussion?

The section 'Professions in Transition' (page 7), discusses developments that will affect the majority of careers in Complementary Medicine. The advice given is general and will apply to almost everybody. Check back to it to see how the discipline that interests you fits into the general picture.

Following the general part of each section, the **Check List** paragraphs suggest ways of looking at what is on offer and deciding whether it will suit your purpose. **Career Planning Factors** lists foreseeable external factors that will impinge on you during your working life. **Working Conditions** describes day to day considerations that may seem trivial but gain in importance when one is working under pressure. Finally **See Also** lists related entries in this book that may suggest a more suitable field or one that can combine with your current skills.

If the subject entries do not show the name you are looking for, consult the Glossary, page 156. Confusion arises because subjects are differently divided and named in different countries and because of a tendency to lift a component skill out of its context, rename it and teach it as a speciality. This last problem is one that arises particularly from contact with the USA. For a number of reasons including the enormous size of the country and the desire to market a service in order to prosper, individuals tend to register brand names for their own speciality. This leads to confusion especially abroad. Where a course is offered in an unfamiliar subject, it is a good idea to check the subjects taught and see whether they form part of something in which reliable standards of training and professional support already exist.

Throughout the book the expression Complementary Medicine is used in the sense understood by the Institute for Complementary Medicine, that is *'health care help that complements the need of the patient'*. This is in no way intended to denigrate the skill and dedication of those who work at the acute and emergency disciplines of medicine and surgery. Here is not the place to enter the often heated discussions between proponents of different terminologies and their political and philosophical implications. The aim of this book is a practical one. If it saves people wasting time on subjects unsuitable to them and directs them to books and institutions that can help them on their way it will have done its job.

Professions in Transition

For those interested in the future wellbeing of people in Britain and in Europe as a whole the present is a time of challenge and opportunity. Two tendencies in attitudes to health that have alternated for the past 200 years seem now to have reached a stage where there can either be a final attempt at mutual elimination or progress to mutual respect and accommodation. This is not the place for extensive historical study but a brief recapitulation may be helpful for those who are planning their career and need a perspective on the entries that follow in the main body of the book.

Vitalism and reductionism

The two attitudes to which I refer are, first, the view generally referred to as '*vitalism*' that living beings have within them a power to resist disease, to recover from trauma and insult of many kinds and to adapt to their surroundings, and, second, the *reductionist* based view that specific phenomena have specific causes and that ill health is best tackled by addressing the specific cause of what is seen to be wrong.

Each of these attitudes has helped patients in the past and each still has much to offer. For example, the victim of a motor accident does indeed need specific and precise repairs to damaged tissue, possibly removal of parts beyond repair and replacement of lost blood to gain time for these repairs to be carried out. It will be noticed here how inevitably one is led to words that might apply almost equally well to the motorist's damaged vehicle. Immediately after the emergency it is the 'reductionist' attitude that will deliver what the patient needs. However, when the surgeons have done their work the patient is left to make what he can of the rest of his life and then what he may well need is help that complements his general needs, physical, emotional, mental and spiritual, rather than targeting one particular part of him.

This book is concerned with opportunities for careers for

people who find that the 'vitalism' attitude most closely matches their own interest in health care.

The connection between standards and methods of training

The range of skills that can be learned is enormous and for a number of historical reasons Britain has available to it some excellent specialised training. High standards in any subject are in fact a national asset and can be a useful invisible export for any nation that fixes them as we have seen in industry where the Deutsche Industrie-Normen (German Industrial Norms) are being adopted by one industry after another throughout the European Community simply because they are so comprehensive and so well worked out.

Traditionally apprenticeship was the way that people in Britain learned their jobs. Because complementary practitioners of the old type exercised skills that received no recognition from society at large, they felt that they were perceived as ignorant quacks and adopted some of the characteristics of a persecuted minority. For instance, many older practitioners felt that they had no right of access to the facilities enjoyed by other professions and groups in society.

This was superseded by training courses taught in colleges, either state or privately run. Most of the people who work in complementary medicine nowadays have been inducted into their work as self-employed practitioners after a training course and probably a period of supervised practice. However, the majority of these courses lead to membership only of an association or register tied to the course in question. Thus pupils are taught, examined and registered by the same people. This has made it extremely difficult for anyone outside the course group to form a reliable idea of the standard of work and for those on the course to have confidence in their own achievements because they have not been measured against an external yardstick.

The quest for establishment

Periodically various of the complementary medical professions have asked the Government to grant them some special status or recognition. However, these requests have always been rejected. Many different reasons can be advanced why this should be so. The lack of clarity of standard has already been mentioned. One may suggest also that the visible tension within many of these professions between the desire for public recognition and the feeling that their art is so esoteric and personal that it cannot be externally defined and assessed makes any progress slow and difficult. This tension has been elegantly analysed by Richenda Power in the case of the osteopathic profession.[1]

Moreover the senior members and governing bodies of the various organisations involved have not helped their case by concentrating their attention on the medical profession and the Department of Health.

To look over one's shoulder at another profession does not suggest self-confidence and independence. Indeed attempts at enlisting the aid of the medical profession are unlikely to serve the interests of the complementary practitioners. Rather it may serve to interest doctors in using the methods themselves. At first sight that might seem an attractive idea, though a damaging one, to many people who have preserved skills through times of neglect and often at considerable sacrifice to themselves. A second glance may be less encouraging. Of course there are doctors who become interested in complementary therapies and decide, in spite of all the pressures on their time and energy, to take a thorough training in the skills that interest them, but the temptation must be there to think that these are very simple skills and can be very quickly learned. It takes great humility to devote the time to learn to do something very simple very well indeed. The length of time that the complementary practitioner takes to train is not only because he has to learn the basic human sciences thoroughly and a body of technical material but because he needs to perfect his skill, be it a hands on physical one or a subtle talking one.

Nor, strangely enough, is the Department of Health necessarily the right target of persuasive efforts. Whenever approached to extend some form of approval to complementary medical professional groupings, the Department has pointed out that its remit is to run the National Health Service as at present constituted, with the

[1] Richenda Power, BA, MSc, *Specialists of the Natural*, 1930–1950 ISBN 1 871695 02 3. Obtainable from Health and Social Research Unit, Department of Social Sciences, Polytechnic of the South Bank, Borough Road, London, SE1 0AA.

implied rider that it is not here to take decisions about what types of health care should be available to the people of the country. Frustration with this stance has perhaps been allowed to distract attention from the fact that the complementary medical professions are in no worse a condition than other types of work in this country.

The status of all jobs in this country

Very few types of work have ever had their scope and content officially determined. In fact this has been a serious disadvantage to many citizens, particularly those who have suffered unemployment. Their skills may be entirely or partly appropriate to the jobs on offer, but unless they can pretend, colourably, to have done exactly that job they will not be considered. Where no job specification exists, there is no possibility of ascertaining and making up the deficit in experience.

Comparison with Europe

This is totally unlike the state of affairs in most other European countries, where the content of any job is ascertainable, specific training exists to supply it and those who have gained the relevant skills are certified as competent to exercise them.

MEASURES TO REMEDY THE DISADVANTAGE TO BRITISH CITIZENS
The prospect of the 'Open Market in Labour' imposed a long overdue change. Plainly if British citizens had no ascertainable qualifications they would have no chance of competing in the Open Market, whereas nationals of other Community countries could come to Britain with clear qualifications to present. To remedy this the Government has charged the National Council for Vocational Qualifications with getting in place definitions of the competences involved in all jobs from the lowest to the highest and interested parties are hastening to fit their activities into the overall scheme.

In sectors where work is predominantly done by employees, it is reasonably clear how to go about fitting workers and employers into the pattern. Complementary practitioners, however, are predominantly self-employed. As such, they have an especial interest in a Directive forthcoming from Brussels on the transfer of the onus of proof of liability for the supply of services. It will be remembered that in Britain caveat emptor has always been the watchword: until recently the buyer always bore the burden of proof that he had been damaged by any product or service that he had bought. This is, of course, becoming unrealistic in an age when the sophistication of many products and services makes it quite impossible for the consumer to know the details of the nature of all the goods and services that he needs. Accordingly a European Community Directive has already become law transferring the onus of proof to the supplier of any product to prove that in all matters under his control he has ensured that it is harmless and fit for its purpose.

A similar Directive, designed to cover the supply of services, is now at the consultative stage. Anyone who wishes to see the papers should apply to the Department of Trade and Industry as soon as possible.

The bearing of this on the self-employed complementary practitioner is plain. It is in his best interests to make as clear as humanly possible to anyone who wishes to use his services exactly what it is that he is offering and what can reasonably be expected.

The British Register of Complementary Practitioners

To facilitate this clarity, the Institute for Complementary Medicine has set up an overall structure called The British Register of Complementary Practitioners.[1] Within this framework individual sections are being set up step by step for different types of complementary medical work. The standards of the different sections will differ as they apply to different types of skill, but they will all be of a level appropriate to clinical work with people who may be seriously ill, rather than at the lower level appropriate to a salon or recreational activity.

METHODS OF DEFINITION
The methods used to define the criteria for entry to the British Register conform wherever possible to those

---

1 This name has been registered with the approval of the Department of Trade and Industry. British and Register are now reserved terms under Community law and can only be used with such approval.

employed by the National Council for Vocational Qualifications so that the complementary therapies can be seen to be setting their house in order.

Contrary to some expectations, the method devised by the National Council for examining and describing the various competences involved in every type of work from dish washing up to the most elevated professions works well for the complementary therapies. A preliminary exercise carried out with members of a range of very different natural therapies tested its capacity to map subjects as various as osteopathy and spiritual healing and showed how effective the method could be in providing a description of even the most personal and spiritual therapies.

BENEFITS ACCRUING FROM THE EXISTENCE OF THE BRITISH REGISTER

As each individual section of the British Register is set up the patient's search to find an appropriate practitioner is made much simpler. Relations between colleagues in different professions are also facilitated as each can be assured that although he does not know what the details of the others' skills may be their membership of a British Register Section guarantees that he can confidently refer patients to them or ask for an authoritative opinion in their proper realms of knowledge. Finally, we can at last look forward to a fruitful period for research as, so far as is possible with the variety in human character and talent, one will be able to specify exactly what is being practised. Research projects until now have often compared results of complementary with orthodox treatment without specifying the background or training of the practitioners. This is as if one mounted a scientific experiment without calibrating the instruments first.

BENEFITS TO TRAINING COLLEGES

Accreditation of colleges and training courses then becomes a simple matter because colleges can know what standards are available to aim for and their arms are much strengthened to resist commercial pressures to reduce length, thoroughness and cost of their courses. It becomes an easily ascertainable matter of fact which colleges and courses have a record of success in preparing pupils for membership of the British Register.

This is not to say that all colleges will want to decide to aim at the same level, but if they wish they can specify clearly that they are, for example, offering a preparatory course and that those who wish to take a full professional course can confidently build on this by adding the advanced material later.

LEVELS OF PROFICIENCY AND PRACTICE APPLICABLE

Some subjects may be taught either at a clinical level appropriate to those aiming to apply for registration with the British Register of Complementary Practitioners or at salon level appropriate to those seeking a career in the Health and Beauty Industry. Once the criteria are well understood, it is possible for people to change their careers and pursue their studies to a more advanced level, possibly after a lapse of time.

Within the professions that are working at clinical level there will of course be considerable overlap in, for example, the knowledge of basic human sciences needed. With definitions of competence in place, a rational system of Credit Accumulation and Transfer becomes a possibility.

INSURANCE FOR PATIENTS AND PRACTITIONERS

Any practitioner joining the British Register is required to be covered by insurance – full professional indemnity and third party liability. Third party liability is also necessary for any clinic or premises in which he may work. This is of course necessary for him to protect himself, but is also an essential protection for his patients.

An additional benefit of the registration scheme which has come as a pleasant surprise has been the improved terms of insurance available to members of the British Register. Actuaries are not interested in the theoretical beauty or benefits to mankind of complementary medicine but only in the risk that it imposes. The British Register is now in its third year and those who are on it have found that, as a result of the record of safety and clear statement of the skills on offer over that time, they can be offered much tighter insurance policies, often at lower rates than they had been paying hitherto. This is not benevolence on the part of the insurers but the results of the logic of the situation.

BENEFITS OF DEFINITIONS TO THE PROFESSIONS

With great labour and against great odds the pioneers in many of the complementary therapies built up their schools and their professional associations. Usually these people were charismatic individuals with tremendous energy and conviction who carried their disciples with them by inspiring deep personal loyalty.

All too often a generation later one would find much of the investment of money and effort dissipated by quarrels reminiscent of church history. Groups of true believers who claimed to teach the true word of the founder would excommunicate heretics who felt that they had developed the truth. These would take their funds and support away to found a new school from the ground up. The effects of the uncertainty and confusion on current pupils and on people in practice can be imagined.

Any means of accommodating change while moderating eccentricity cannot but help to reduce the personal distress and waste of effort and resources caused by these natural political developments within professions. From time to time under the descriptions of particular types of career reference will be made to provisions for continuing career development and supervision relationships. These, combined with the template definitions provided by the various sections of the British Register, should allow flexibility and growth and make it unnecessary for people to feel so constrained that they must cut themselves off from their colleagues.

THE SUB-DIVISION OF SUBJECTS AND THE PERIL OF THE BRAND NAME

Britain and Ireland have been particularly vulnerable over the past few years to incursions from overseas by people offering training courses in subjects with impressive and unfamiliar names. These, often expensive, courses are usually advertised as intensives. This word can sometimes be a warning signal to examine what is on offer very carefully.

If it denotes a series of concentrated seminars for people already active in a profession, well and good. If it concerns a proposal to turn out a qualified practitioner in short order, examine it carefully. If it concerns a subject with an unfamiliar name, again, ask for clear definitions. It may turn out that the new subject is merely a sub-division of part of the skills usually taught in one of the established professions given a new name.

Names are commercially important because they can be registered as brands. Where this has happened, more often in the United States of America than in Britain, considerable sums can be made by someone who has registered an attractive name for some quite normal and well understood skill. The brand name is publicised, its owner is interviewed on the media, the public feel sure this must be something really important and the pressure is on many perfectly competent practitioners to go on a course (intensive, of course) that will get them a certificate with the coveted brand name on it.

Who are the practitioners?

The stereotype of a natural therapist used to be of an uneducated person who practised in isolation, almost in secret, who learned his skills (usually described as mumbo-jumbo) by a system of apprenticeship and preyed on the weak and the gullible, particularly rich, elderly women. This stereotype dies hard, surviving like other traditional myths within the conventions of popular comedy. A regular slot on the Ken Dodd Show used to have a rustic-accented practitioner inviting a patient into the kitchen at the dark of the moon. The punch line, after instructions about preparations of nettles and various other ingredients, turned out to be 'and then take all your clothes off, my dear.'

This appalling caricature has probably never been totally true, but it is worth examining the constituent elements and comparing them with the present state of affairs.

Many modern practitioners have completed a university degree before beginning their professional training. This is predominantly so in the main therapies. Others have re-trained in mid-life and already hold professional qualifications. They are thus likely to be mature in years and, it is to be hoped, in personality. Complementary medicine is one field where maturity is a positive advantage. In August, 1990, for example, ICM staff gave career advice to a tax accountant turned McTimoney Chiropractor, a school headmaster who became an aromatherapist, a marine biologist who had retrained as a neuro-muscular masseur, a pharmacist who sought information about training in herbal medicine. These are hardly uncouth ignoramuses.

The skills involved in complementary disciplines are often subtle, but they involve a considerable amount of learning, both theoretical and practical. Full professional courses are taught and examined in both aspects and underpinned by what might be called basic sciences such as anatomy and physiology at appropriate levels.

THREE MAIN PATTERNS OF TRAINING

The professions listed in the later pages will mostly be seen to fall into three main patterns.

For the 'Big Five' subjects, Acupuncture, Chiropractic, Herbal Medicine, Homoeopathy, and Osteopathy, one should be looking at a course approximating to degree standard. In some cases courses taught by particular colleges have already achieved recognition and degrees are awarded to successful candidates. Other colleges teaching the same subjects to the same standards of excellence may simply be awarding their own diplomas. This should not be taken to mean that their work or the competence of their graduates is necessarily in any way inferior. It is to be hoped that work now going forward with the British Register of Complementary Practitioners and with the National Council for Vocational Qualifications will make it possible to expand, rather than restrict, the number of ways in which it is possible for the practitioners of the future to achieve recognition. Entrants are usually expected to have two science A levels and many have already completed a degree course of some kind. This can make difficulties for the entrant, especially in obtaining finance, but should be seen from the point of view of the standards of the professions involved as an advantage. People with many different kinds of academic background have much to offer. Arts graduates and practitioners, in particular, enrich the therapies in which they engage. It is time that we discarded the idea that the arts do not provide a rigorous training. On the contrary, linguistic and philosophical studies, for example, are excellent in precisely the sort of rigorous discussion of assumptions that is essential to fruitful scientific effort. Practitioners with a background in the performing arts are particularly strong in the skills of communication and empathy which are vital in therapies where the patient is being invited to examine his feelings, receive and respond to new information and perhaps radically alter his lifestyle.

For candidates lacking a scientific background an Access or Conversion course can be helpful.

Once trained, the newly qualified practitioners are expected to work under supervision for a specified period before launching into independent practice.

Other subjects fall within Diploma (two years) or Certificate (one year) and may be practised in their own right or as adjuncts to other skills.

THE PHYSICAL SETTING

Few practitioners nowadays invite patients into their kitchens. Although some have their practice room in their own home or adjoining it, as used until very recently to be the case with general practitioner doctors and with dentists, many more now use professional practice rooms managed by a commercial enterprise that provides all the necessary facilities for laundry, cleaning, reception and so on for a group of different practitioners. Practitioners themselves and their professional organisations insist on the maintenance of the highest standards of hygiene. Indeed, one of the criticisms of modern high tech medicine is that it requires patients to risk cross infection in huge hospitals where reliance on antibiotics has eroded standards of hygiene and bred strains of super-bugs resistant to the drugs supposed to control them. This is contrasted, by the proponents of the natural therapies, with their own stress on cleanliness and healthy living conditions.

THE SKILLS OFFERED

Far from picking a few nettles and random weeds to throw in a cauldron, the modern medical herbalist will have access to plant material from sources all over the world, grown to a set standard, and will have studied their pharmacological action in detail. Increasingly he may in fact already be a pharmacist who knows at first hand the perils of the modern pharmacopoeia and is interested in offering his customers the riches of the Green Pharmacy.

THE ETHICAL FRAMEWORK

The sexual suggestiveness of the invitation to 'take off all your clothes, my dear' is equally inappropriate to the work of complementary therapists. Many of the natural therapies which are concerned with the mind and emotions rather than the body do not require *any* physical contact with the patient, let alone the sort of physical examination requiring the removal of clothes. In the manual therapies and those that require physical examination of the patient, the ways in which this should be done are clearly laid down by the codes of ethics and practice by which practitioners are governed. The following quotation from the codes of practice for the Classical Homoeopathic Division of the British Register of Complementary Practitioners is typical of the behaviour expected:

3. Homoeopathic Practitioners may not:

a) *use the title 'Doctor' unless they are registered physicians with the Medical Association in the country of practice. Further, if a treatment is offered to a patient which is not that in which the Practitioner holds a qualification or doctorate they shall so inform the patient;*

b) *address or refer to an assistant as 'Nurse' unless said assistant holds a nursing qualification in the country in which the practitioner is operating the clinic;*

c) *conduct a physical examination of a child under 16 years of age except in the presence of a parent or guardian or other responsible adult;*

d) *conduct a genital examination of a patient without a chaperon being present unless written consent has been given;*

e) *make any written or oral claim for treatment of any given disease.*

Similarly careful consideration is of course given to emotional and many other issues where appropriate.

USE OF TITLES

The sensitive matter of the use of the word doctor is addressed in this section of the code in question. An increasing number of practitioners in fact possess doctorates from universities or polytechnics and are thus truly entitled to the appellation doctor which is given as a courtesy title to medical people. Nevertheless, in order to prevent any suggestion of confusion, most of these people prefer to call themselves Mr or Ms N, PhD and in many cases their professional code enjoins this. This is perhaps enough to dissipate the misconceptions about the practitioner.

What of the patient?

The *Survey of Trends in Complementary Medicine*, published by the Institute for Complementary Medicine in 1984, is one of the few factual sources available on the subject. Peter Davies, PhD asked practitioners who were members of reputable professional associations to consult the case notes in their files and answer a number of questions about their patients, the course of treatments and their own training. It emerged that the patients were overwhelmingly people in the prime years of their working life. This suggested that they were not, as popular superstition would have it, the weak and the gullible of the population, but people at their most active and vital, interested in remaining fit for their busy lives and seeking help to do so from those qualified in skills operating on the borderlands where the physical, the mental, the emotional and the spiritual aspects of life meet.

The *British Medical Journal* of 26th January, 1991, summarises the results of a survey of the whole field of alternative medicine that it commissioned from Sheffield University. Although the questions that were asked and the aim of the survey were different, the conclusions about the users of the complementary therapies seem to have broadly confirmed those of the earlier survey.

Mori and Mintel Public Opinion Polls during 1990 confirmed that 75 percent of respondents wished to see complementary medicine available on the same terms as National Health Service treatments, that is without extra charge to the patient at the time of use.

Practitioners maintain complete professional confidentiality about the problems and identity of those that they treat, but, again taking the information from the file of enquiries received from the general public at the Institute for Complementary Medicine, referrals during the past few months to complementary medical practitioners included people from the following occupations: public relations officer, local authority employee, heavy goods vehicle driver, housewife, teacher, taxi driver, police officer, dancer, higher civil servant, minister of religion, career adviser, shop assistant, farmer, social worker, retired naval officer, unemployed, businessman, laboratory worker, librarian. These happened to be cases where the occupation of the enquirer was mentioned because it was relevant to the problem with which they sought help. Many more did not feel it relevant to mention their field of work.

These last two paragraphs point to a source of distortion in the use of complementary practitioner services. The enquiries came from people across the whole socio-economic spectrum. The actual use, though the social background is not always recorded, seems to be predominantly by those with the disposable funds to pay. One should note that this is not equivalent to rich, but describes merely those whose incomes are not totally absorbed by the barest necessities for existence. The Institute for Complementary Medicine believes that provisions to prevent people being denied access to the help of complementary practitioners on economic grounds are overdue and can be simply arranged.

As well as those of English, Irish, Scottish and Welsh origin, visitors from many countries and British nationals of African, Chinese, Indian, Moroccan, Pakistani, West Indian and various European heritages have used the Institute for Complementary Medicine's referral system. One interesting suggestion is that people who have moved between cultures and had effective help with health matters from people who work within differing theoretical frameworks are apt to be open minded about unfamiliar approaches.

It seems to be the case that the people who consult complementary medical practitioners, far from being a group of cranks, are normal people representative of the population from which they come.

The effect of gender

Every study on record has shown up a surplus of women

over men among users of complementary medicine. So far
the reasons for this have not been clearly identified, though
three main theories are generally proposed.

1   Women use more of all medical and care systems than
men. Therefore their use of complementary medical
services merely reflects their use of medical and care systems
in general. Perhaps one should balance this suggestion with
the thought that women are also large providers of informal
care within society and that therefore much male use of care
services goes unrecorded because the provision has been
made by wives or other female relations.

2   Women's needs are poorly served by orthodox medical
provision. This is supported by a great deal of rhetoric
because of its political implications, but its testing requires
the framing of clearer definitions and criteria than have yet
been applied.

3   Women act as scouts for the family and will show up as
an apparent surplus in all situations where they are
investigating or shopping, whether it be for health services,
clothes, food, household equipment or any other family
needs. This seems to be born out by market research and is
appealing from an anthropological point of view, as it seems
to suggest that in spite of modern perceptions of changing
gender roles, women are maintaining their traditional
functions. In so-called hunter-gatherer societies, the men
ceremonially engage in hunting expeditions that produce
infrequent feasts of meat, whereas the women provide the
staples of life by gathering activities analogous to shopping.
Feminists point with amusement to the important and high
status world of employment as analogous to the male
hunting activity compared with the unrewarded work that
maintains family life.

A pattern for the future

Our hope is that recognition of registered practitioners will
lead to a situation where they can occupy the same sort of
position in relation to General Practitioners as do dentists, so
that, rather than practitioners being ordered to apply
certain treatments, patients will be recommended to enquire
whether the complementary practitioner is able to suggest

helpful treatment. With control of budgets increasingly being delegated, it may then be possible for treatment costs to be reimbursed in the same way as drug costs. Obviously it is important to note that the public must not be deprived of the right to direct access to the complementary practitioner. Referral must be freely possible in both directions. This may seem an impossible ideal in present conditions, but 1990 saw the defeat by only three votes of a motion in the House of Lords to make complementary medicine available on the National Health Service. The strength of the political will for this important reform will not surprise anyone closely connected with the field, though it undoubtedly came as a shock to many observers.

Update yourself on local conditions

Within the next few months changes will have taken place that make it impossible to give exact advice at present. Anyone planning a career in complementary medicine will need to check the latest information and see how it applies to him. Two areas will be particularly affected.

1   The British Register of Complementary Practitioners will be opening divisions for different types of practice. Enquire if there is one available for your subject and if there is ask for registration papers, so as to see what is required. This will provide a useful checklist of what to look for when seeking a training course. If in doubt, ask which courses are likely to be successful in preparing you for registration.

2   The Department of Employment's Manpower Commission, which became the Training Agency, has now been devolved into locally based Training and Enterprise Councils (TECs). These rapid changes must be as confusing for the people involved as they are for everyone else. We cannot yet know what will be the outcome, though plainly it is hoped that the TECs will be able to be responsive to local need. This presumably means that they will not be uniform in their view of their functions or of the merits of training plans. It will be essential to make contact with the local TEC to ascertain what attitude it takes to supporting with grants or career development loans training courses in the natural therapies.

Acupuncture

 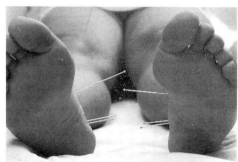

Needle in position for a patient with skin problems and high blood pressure.

The Acupuncturist chooses the exact pattern of needle positions for the patient's problem.

Acupuncture is one of the skills in which professional Chinese Medicine practitioners are trained. It is based on the idea that there are lines of force (meridians) dividing the human body into zones and that needling, pressure or burning of moxa on specific points on these lines can have beneficial effects on health by regulating the flow of vital energy. The perceived facts on which it is based are obviously related to other types of practice such as reflexology and zone therapy developed in the Western world.

Within Britain there are many organisations offering training in acupuncture and acupressure, the main differences being the degree to which they set the teaching of the skill within the theory of Chinese medicine and the amount of understanding of western medical sciences considered appropriate for a practitioner of acupuncture.

Personality

A mature personality balancing apparently opposite characteristics is needed. Flexible willingness to learn should go with an intelligently questioning attitude. A considerable amount of rote learning is involved so patience and strength of motivation are important. Practice involves both physical contact with patients and reference to a highly abstract system of theory. The tutor will also need to judge whether the candidate is capable of the fine co-ordination of hand and eye necessary for developing acupuncture skills.

Those who decide to study with a native Chinese should decide whether they have the patience and persistence to accept a teaching style that may be unfamiliar and uncongenial to them. Westerners are accustomed to a lively and supportive teaching style where questions are encouraged and pupils are given reasons for each step. Traditional teachers may seem authoritarian and can often impose repeated practice of detailed skills on which the pupil is expected to reflect without question. Explanations may be supplied later. Traditionally the pupil served his master during his training and counted this as a privilege.

Education

Most people undertaking training, but by no means all, start with a degree nowadays. A level equivalent education is the minimum. Many successful acupuncturists come from backgrounds such as physiotherapy or nursing, seeking for explanations of some of the phenomena they have encountered in their practice. This means that they have already absorbed orthodox teaching of anatomy and some physiology and pathology which is an advantage.

Access

Provided they have the essential educational background, candidates are usually further selected for training by interview. Tutors will be looking for people with the personal characteristics outlined above.

Career development

Course length varies according to the theoretical framework as outlined above and the previous background of the candidates. For instance, The Academy of Western Acupuncture trains doctors, dentists, physiotherapists and SRNs in formula acupuncture using only Western diagnosis. Licentiate in Acupuncture is gained after one year part time and higher qualifications after a further three years part time.

Courses that train people without previous medical background tend to take three years to bring pupils to licentiate level, usually giving lectures and practical training at weekends and demanding a considerable amount of home study. Higher qualifications can then be worked for, usually by part-time two-year courses while the licentiate is starting in practice.

Working conditions

The newly trained acupuncturist will normally work under supervision of a senior practitioner while preparing for higher qualifications. This applies whether he or she is a qualified paramedical person or a specialist who started training without previous medical experience. Two years is usually spent gaining experience in this way.

Thereafter the usual conditions of freelance private practice apply, with a few added problems specific to acupuncturists. Since the coming of AIDS the public has rightly been extremely conscious of the need for hygiene and acupuncturists are seen as presenting a distinct risk by some local authorities. This is unreasonable as their training includes strict rules about needle cleanliness and instruction on the use of the autoclave. In fact, practitioners nowadays use disposable needles which come in sterilised packs. However, the feeling that there is a doubt in the mind of the local authority staff is one factor that may decide acupuncturists to forgo the convenience and informality of working at home for the professionalism of hiring a room in a practice suite on a sessional basis. In exchange for the sessional rent the provider of the service takes off the practitioner's shoulders the problems of rent, unified business rate, third party liability insurance, cleaning and reception. The practitioner of course is responsible for maintaining his professional indemnity, so that he is covered against malpractice or negligence claims.

CHECK LIST

- Is the course of the level and type that you want or will you need to go elsewhere later to expand your knowledge and experience?
- Are you simply trying to learn a physical skill or do you want to learn the total Chinese approach to health? In

which case consult the section on *Chinese Medicine.*
- Does the training course have a connection with a Chinese teaching hospital? Do you need to take a preparatory or access course in order to make the best use of the course material?
- Has the training organisation applied for validation, or is the diploma accredited by a professional body or learned institute other than itself? What resources does the training organisation make available to you – libraries – study rooms – different specialist staff – individualised tuition for individual learning problems – pastoral counselling on personal matters?
- Can the tutorial staff put you in touch with former students who can give you a retrospective view of the course?
- Are there opportunities for further personal and career development?

Career planning factors

Advantageous
With increased contact between East and West acupuncture and other Oriental skills are no longer seen as eccentric or incredible. More people are seeking the help of acupuncturists and hearing of its usefulness in a wide range of health problems.

Disadvantageous
Over the next few years it is likely that there will be growing numbers of Chinese visitors qualified in acupuncture competing with British trainees for patients.

What research has been undertaken in this country has often been done by doctors who have completed short courses. The lack of standardisation in skill and the concentration on pain control to the exclusion of other properties of acupuncture may cast doubt on the usefulness of the results.

Finance

Discretionary grants are available from some local authorities for professional courses, particularly where the candidate has the backing of a relevant respected local body or national organisation, but you will be dependent on the amount of money available at any one time and on the opinions of the grants committee. Candidates who already have a degree or professional training may be felt to have used up their entitlement to public support. Applications showing the desired training as a logical and necessary career step are most likely to be favourably received. Obtain a place on a course before making application.

Useful addresses

Academy of Chinese Acupuncture, 15–17 Southend Road, London, NW3   071–794–0848
Tuition from Chinese doctor in the Chinese system.
Academy of Western Acupuncture, 12 Rodney Street, Liverpool, L1   051–709–0479
Linked with Association of Western Acupuncture. Medical and paramedical personnel only within the framework of Western medicine.
International College of Oriental Medicine, Green Hedges House, Green Hedges Avenue, East Grinstead, Sussex RH19 1DZ   0342–313106/7
Linked with International Register of Oriental Medicine.
London School of Acupuncture and Traditional Chinese Medicine, 3rd floor, 36 Featherstone Street, London EC1Y 8QX   071–490–0513

Books

Ewald, Dr Hans 1978, *Acupressure Techniques*, Thorsons, London.
Veith, I trans. 1986, *The Yellow Emperor's Classic of Internal Medicine (Nei Ching)*, University of California Press.
Needham, J. & Gwei-Djen, L. 1980, *Celestial Lancets: A History and Rationale of Acupuncture and Moxa*, Cambridge University Press.
Kapchuk, T. 1984, *The Web that Has No Weaver*, Hutchinson, London.

See also
Chinese Medicine, Reflexology, Shiatsu, *Zone Therapy*

Alexander Technique

*The Alexander Technique is named after its inventor,
F.M. Alexander, an actor who developed a method of re-training
himself in the right use of his body and voice after experiencing a
number of professional disappointments which he attributed to
learned habits of faulty posture.*

*Actors, musicians and dancers are still among those who find the
technique most helpful, though its scope has been extended by later
teachers to a much wider range of problems connected with posture
and physical habits. Pupils testify to the emotional and psychological
benefits that they feel they have derived from their improved use of
their bodies.*

*Enthusiasts point out that the human species has only developed
the habit of walking on the hind legs fairly recently in its evolution
and that this posture makes great demands on the joints, the muscles
and the cardiovascular system.*

*Traditionally the leaders of the movement have denied that they
are practising a therapy and laid great stress on the view that they
are teachers of a technique. The emphasis is on general improvement
in the use of the body from which correction of individual detailed
faults will follow. However, to train as a teacher of the Alexander
Technique requires the candidate to learn much that is common to a
number of the natural therapies.*

Personality

Ideally, the person who will make a good Alexander
Teacher will combine an artistic interest in physical self-
expression with a scientific interest in anatomy, physiology
and psychology. If you are going to help performing artists
it is especially helpful if you have experience of their
particular art, so that you can quickly come to an
understanding of its demands on the body and mind as well
as the emotions.

Education

A level or equivalent education is probably the minimum to
which anyone who wishes to train as an Alexander Teacher
should add experience of the technique as a trainee. In fact

many people who have already completed a medical or artistic education take up the subject, often as a result of personal problems.

Alexander Teachers need to learn more anatomy, physiology and pathology than they are likely ever to use in their own practice because they are in contact with the public who may bring them pathological problems that should be recognised and referred elsewhere.

Practical experience in one of the performing arts can also be a great help. A violinist, for example, who knows by experience the problems that can arise from the physical demands of the instrument will grasp at once material that can present difficulties to people without such experience.

Access

Candidates are usually selected for training by interview after the suitability of their education and experience has been ascertained. Tutors will be looking for people who are alert, observant of detail, outgoing and physically expressive.

Career development

Teachers develop their practice through the Society of Teachers of the Alexander Technique (STAT) who perform the valuable function of directing new pupils to those teachers who have space available for them. The Society also acts as a professional forum and puts on post-qualification workshops and other functions. Through the Society teachers can keep in touch with colleagues and develop their ideas. They may be invited to join in training the next generation of teachers.

As has been suggested, many teachers have special links with particular arts and will wish to specialise their practice in these areas. Thus many colleges of music have Alexander teachers among their staff or attached to the college more or less formally.

Courses are generally arranged over three years of three 12 week terms during which 20 hours a week are class work. This fits the Department of Education definition of a full-time course. Even so some trainees find that it is possible to continue working while learning.

In a loosely organised subject such as this there is no rigid hierarchy of promotion and the burden of administration tends to be left to conscientious and enthusiastic individuals. Senior teachers ultimately teach the next generation. There are still a few people alive who were taught by F.M. Alexander himself. It remains to be seen how the subject will develop when this generation passes away.

Working conditions

Teachers of Alexander Technique take individual pupils or small classes. For both space is desirable, so teaching will probably take place in a large room or small hall or gymnasium. This requirement makes it useful to have a connection with a college or other organisation that may be able to offer suitable space or to team up with colleagues to use hired space to the best advantage.

Many teachers combine their Alexander Teaching with another career.

Check List

- Pay particular attention to the personality specifications and decide whether you can maintain the necessary levels of physical energy to inspire pupils who are suffering professional discouragement and physical pain.
- Have you the physical and mental stamina to run parallel careers? Some people find the need to switch between different modes of thought and expression stimulating. For others it is confusing and tiring.

Career planning factors

Advantageous

The demand for teaching remains steady.

This is a useful additional string to the bow of anyone, particularly women, whose career is likely to be broken by the demands of family life.

STAT gives useful support in building a list of pupils.

Disadvantageous
The subject occupies an anomalous position, not quite a
therapy, not quite a science, which may hamper future
developments.

Finance

Discretionary grants are available from some local
authorities for professional courses, particularly where the
candidate has the backing of a relevant respected local body
or national organisation, but you will be dependent on the
amount of money available at any one time and on the
opinions of the grants committee. Candidates who already
have a degree or professional training may be felt to have
used up their entitlement to public support. Applications
showing the desired training as a logical and necessary
career step are most likely to be favourably received. Obtain
a place on a course before making application.

Useful addresses

The Alexander Institute, 16 Balderton Street,
London W1   071–408–2384
Contact Dr Barlow.

The Alexander Teaching Centre, 188 Old Street, London
EC1V 9BP   071–250–3038

The Centre for the Alexander Technique, 46 Stevenage
Road, London SW6   071–731–6348
Contact Mrs E. Ribeaux.

The Centre for Development in Alexander Technique,
142 Thorpedale Road, London N4

The Constructive Teaching Centre, 18 Lansdowne Road,
London W11 3LL   071–727–7222
Contact Mr Carrington.

Mcdonald Training Course for the Alexander Technique,
50A Belgrave Road, London SW1   071–821–7916
Contact Mr P.J. Macdonald.

The New Alexander School, 21 Lyndhurst Road,
Hampstead NW3 5NX   071–435–4321

Contact Mr R. Simmons.

North London Alexander School, 10 Elmcroft Avenue, London NW11   081–455–3938
Contact M.M. Magidov.

School of Alexander Studies, 44 Park Avenue North, London, NW8   081–348–5054

Alexander Technique Training Centre, Community College, Fore St., Totnes, Devon TQ9 5RP   0803–864218
Contact Mrs A. Haahr.

The Society of Teachers of Alexander Technique, 10 London House, 266 Fulham Road, London, SW6 071–351–0828
Contact Miss C. Langhorn who keeps addresses of approved teachers throughout the country.

Books

Alexander, F.M. 1971, *The Resurrection of the Body*, Dell, New York.
          and 1985 *The Uses of the Self*, Gollancz, London.

Barlow, W. 1982, *The Alexander Principle*, Gollancz, London.

Jones, F.P. 1976, *Body Awareness in Action: A study of the Alexander Technique*, Schocken, New York.

See also
Feldenkrais Technique

Anthroposophical Medicine

Anthroposophy is a system of thought based on the ideas of the German mystic Rudolph Steiner. As he had views on all subjects from architecture through child development to physics, he naturally also developed a way of thinking about medicine.

Some of his views can be traced to the influence of the poet Goethe while others use ideas close to those of Hahnemann, the founder of homoeopathy.

As well as strictly medical work, there are possibilities to train in artistic therapy, eurhythmy and speech therapy within the anthroposophical system.

Personality

The world of Anthroposophy is composed of people who know that their views differ from those of the majority of their compatriots. This has both rewards and penalties. Those who wish to use only anthroposophical medicine run in this country no danger except that of being thought to be cranky. A doctor who wishes to practise should consider whether he can take the pressure that may be exerted on him by his professional colleagues, who can be tolerant of many things but very tough indeed with those who are felt to have overstepped the bounds.

Education

Although anyone is able to study Steiner's ideas, the practice of anthroposophical medicine is only open to those who have already undertaken a medical training. The basic conditions are therefore those that apply to the training of doctors.

Access

Only doctors are admitted as anthroposophical doctors. Candidates are usually selected for training by interview. A foundation course in anthroposophical thought is offered at Emerson College. People who have taken part as staff or volunteers in anthroposophical educational or other projects will be in the best position to fit in.

Other types of therapist also start with a foundation course at Emerson College.

Career development

We have suggested that anthroposophical practitioners may find that they are subject to professional pressures. Anyone who proposes to follow this course must be aware that it may be difficult to fit in with the general organisation of the medical service in this country. The doctor practising under the National Health Service should certainly consult his Area Health Authority and senior professional colleagues before making any decision. It may be that private practice is the only way in which he can deliver this type of help to patients who desire it.

If he decides that he can only satisfy himself by practising privately, there are obvious disadvantages in terms of professional advancement. Many interesting connections and posts of great importance will be closed to him. However, in compensation, he may find it possible to join up with some of the medical and educational organisations run by the Anthroposophical movement and develop a satisfying career with congenial colleagues.

In Germany and some other European countries anthroposophical medicine is more commonly practised and the free market in labour should mean increased opportunities for doctors who have this bent and would like to work elsewhere in the European Community.

Artistic therapy training takes two and a half years.

A Diploma in art therapy can be taken in conjunction with existing courses noted under the heading of *Art Therapy*. Total joint course time is three years.

Diploma in curative eurhythmy can be gained through a four year course followed by one year of supervised practice.

Working conditions

These will be dictated by the considerations we have outlined above. Clinics run as part of charitable foundations vary enormously in the scale and quality of their provision. In private practice the doctor will be providing and controlling his own surroundings even more than he would as a general practitioner within the National Health Service. He will need to take positive steps to make sure that he does not allow himself to become socially and professionally isolated.

The Anthroposophical Medical Association runs a regular programme of study days, members' conferences and study conferences.

CHECK LIST

If you are already a convinced anthroposophist you will be aware of the ideas and atmosphere of this orientation. The options and theories you should check are those in the wider world. See whether you can fulfill your ideals without isolating yourself from what your colleagues will regard as the mainstream of your profession.

- Check that the training you are contemplating can be used as widely as possible. Enquire about links with other anthroposophical bodies in the countries of the European Community and possibilities of professional visits and exchanges with them.
- What resources does the training organisation make available to you – libraries – personal counselling – study rooms – different specialist staff? How do these compare with equivalent courses and resources in normal academic courses in parallel subjects.
- Can the tutorial staff put you in touch with former students who can give you a retrospective view of the course?
- Can you meet former students and see how their training has worked out in terms of the practice and job opportunities available to them?

Career planning factors

Advantageous

Anthroposophical medicine is gentle and does not involve the practitioner in many of the conventional activities that are repugnant to practitioners and patients alike.

Disadvantageous
Only those factors suggested above. The rewards of
conventional medicine are so considerable that they should
not be lightly forgone.

Finance

The Anthroposophical Society has some funds available to
support projects and can put new practitioners in touch with
sources of loans specifically earmarked for health or other
socially beneficial schemes.

Useful addresses

Anthroposophical Medical Association, c/o Rudolf Steiner
House, 35 Park Road, London NW1 6XT
071–723–4400

The Anthroposophical Society, Rudolf Steiner House, 35
Park Road, London NW1 6XT   071–723–4400
*This is the first point of reference for all types of therapeutic practice.
They can direct you to individual anthroposphical training
organisations and institutions.*

Park Attwood, Trimpley, Nr Bewdley, Gloucestershire
*Park Attwood is the movement's nursing home where
anthroposophical treatments are available. It is rare for
complementary medical treatments to be available in a residential
setting.*

Books

Steiner, Rudolf 1948, *Spiritual Science and Medicine*, Rudolf
Steiner Press, London.

Bott, Victor 1978, *Anthroposophical Medicine*, Rudolf Steiner
Press, London.

See also
Art Therapy, **Homoeopathy**, **Psychotherapy**

Aromatherapy

Aromatherapy may be offered at different levels of skill and knowledge. Some people mistakenly believe aromatherapy to be merely the application of perfume to the body by means of massage or scented baths. Such an experience may be pleasant but is not what is properly meant by aromatherapy. Properly understood this is an attempt to improve the patient's state by stimulating the receptor cells of the body by a very precise use of aromatic essences. These cells then send messages via the deepest levels of the brain to tell the whole person how to get well. This is particularly effective where illnesses have an element of mood and emotion.

France is the country in which the practice has been most highly developed in modern times. The biochemistry underlying the subject is by no means fully understood though forthcoming French publications are believed to present a more complete account of the scientific background than has been available before.

Skilled practitioners use a range of 40 or more different aromatic essences according to very specific chemical indications and their own initiative and inventiveness to devise suitable ways of delivering them to the patients.

Personality

A range of all-round talents is needed for the practice of aromatherapy. Physically one needs sensitive organs of smell comparable with those possessed by the perfumer's nose or the winemaker's palate. Any adequate training should give a sound scientific basis for the work and practical skills in its use but the ideal entrant for training will bring a talent for empathy with the feelings of others that can be developed during the course.

Education

Background knowledge of human anatomy, physiology and pathology are obviously useful. It is tempting to add biochemistry but the problem is that the subject where it applies to this therapy has been developed overwhelmingly in the direction of synthesising commercial flavourings and pharmaceuticals. Work written in France and not yet available in translation may prove to have filled in some of the gaps. One is dealing here with a subject that is not thoroughly understood and there is therefore no ideal educational path by which to approach it.

Access

Access to the subject will vary among the different courses on offer and when comparing them one should take into account the assumptions that they make about what entrants know already. For example, massage is one way of applying aromatic essences. This has led to widespread confusion in the public mind that aromatherapy *is* massage with aromatic oils. Some courses are constructed on the assumption that everyone joining will already be aware of human anatomy and capable of giving a general body massage. Others assume that these subjects will need to be taught. Similarly the treatment of the material that is specifically to do with aromatherapy is very different between one course and another. Some simply list a number of aromatic essences and tell pupils what health problems they may be used for. Others attempt, so far as the scientific knowledge is available, to give a deeper understanding of the reasons for choosing one rather than another, so that the pupil is equipped to deal with unforeseen problems and to follow the developments of the subject as they appear. Probably the best advice at present is to seek the course that is most likely to equip you with the knowledge and skills to become an independent practitioner even if gaining access to it means first upgrading your knowledge and skills in supporting subjects.

Career development

Opportunities vary widely. There are now aromatherapists working in private practice, in intensive care units, in hospices, in geriatric units, with the disabled in day care centres and in many other settings. Private practice is, however, the most reliable of these from the point of view of the practitioner because, difficult though it may be, it is within his or her own control. All too often the very welcome contributions within the National Health Service are unofficial and done as part of a nurse's general activities. This means that the aromatherapy is treated as something that can be done if the nurse has the time and is therefore pursued inconsistently, is a volunteer activity, is not properly recorded so that the results can not be audited, or can be discontinued or forbidden at the whim of anyone in authority who may be uninformed or uninterested. There are, however, signs of change. For example, the decision has recently been taken by Hillingdon Health Authority to employ a full time aromatherapist for hospitals in their district. This shows movement in the right direction as the person in the post will be there specifically as an aromatherapist rather than either as a volunteer from outside or as a nurse who happens to have some useful extra skill.

Nurses show great interest in the subject and it is one that offers them a career path that makes sense both within the National Health Service and when they wish to work for a period outside it. A number of courses specifically designed for their needs are now being mounted by the established colleges and it is hoped that there will soon be a possibility of formal accreditation.

Given proper attention to the problem of labelling this is a career suitable for the blind.

An Aromatherapy Division of the British Register of Complementary Practitioners will shortly open for applications. Anyone who would like to have application forms sent should write specifying the subject they are interested in and enclosing a large stamped self-addressed envelope.

Working conditions

As indicated above these vary widely.

In private practice great attention should be given to avoiding the massage parlour image, so that the practitioner should seek a practice room that is warm and welcoming but highly professional.

Many patients who are elderly or convalescent would welcome a visiting service at home and this can be an excellent way of establishing rapport and making a first hand assessment of social factors that may affect the patient's progress. Practitioners contemplating this type of work should contact the Suzy Lamplugh Trust, 14 East Sheen Avenue, London SW14, Tel.: 081–392–1839 for advice on how to be safety conscious but not paranoid.

Nurses with specialisations are well placed to drive the subject forward by investigating its relevance to their particular interests once they have trained. For example, there are many reports of the usefulness of aromatherapy in improving mood, a simple research project based on records kept by nurses in wards could provide the sort of basic data that can lead to much more detailed studies and provide valuable information for use both by practitioners and by patients on a self-help basis.

When patients are seriously ill or weak, the practitioner's help is essential and it is always advisable that he or she should be in the background to monitor progress but a rewarding aspect of the work is teaching the patient how to use some basic materials. This needs to be done within a framework of safeguards to prevent misuse of powerful essences and overconfidence.

CHECK LIST

- Have you the temperament to live with a subject that is not yet fully developed and grow with it as more substantiated knowledge becomes available?
- Can you resist the temptation to make easy money by using inferior perfumed material rather than the very expensive organic essences?

Career planning factors

Advantageous

This is a highly portable skill. Any equipment is small and light. A kit of essences can be carried in a small unbreakable case. Supplies can be despatched through the post in padded bags.

The precious essences are used in tiny quantities. There is therefore little difficulty in holding and storing stock under suitable conditions.

For people with a scientific bent there are opportunities for original research.

The subject has a delightful public image and can lead to interesting opportunities in the media.

The connection with growers of the various aromatic plants and spices can lead to fascinating opportunities for travel or development of business.

Disadvantageous

As suggested above there can be confusion with businesses providing perfumes and beauty products. Practitioners may need to make it very clear what level of service they are providing.

For some people the gaps in the scientific underpinning may appear to be a threat rather than an opportunity.

Finance

Unlikely to be available from Education Authorities. Training and re-training schemes, which vary very much from place to place, are more likely to be helpful as the training can be seen as a means of placing candidates in self-employment. Seek advice from any Local Enterprise organisations and bear in mind the possibility of obtaining a career development loan.

Useful addresses

Association of Tisserand Aromatherapists, 3 Shirley Street, Hove, East Sussex BN3 3WI   0273–772479/706640

Institute of Biomedical Sciences, 15 Approach Road, London SW20 8BA   081–543–7633
Contact: Mrs Frances Clifford.

Natural By Nature Oils Limited, 27 Vivian Avenue, Hendon Central, London NW4 3UX   081–202–5718

Books

Tisserand, Robert 1977, *The Art of Aromatherapy*, C.W. Daniel, Saffron Walden, Essex.

Valnet, Jean 1980, *The Practice of Aromatherapy*, C.W. Daniel,

Saffron Walden, Essex.

See also
Herbal Medicine, **Hypnotherapy**, **Psychotherapy**

Art Therapy

Art has been used therapeutically for much of human history. Indeed, one may view many of the art treasures of the past in shrines, icons and devotional objects as having therapeutic value to the beholders. Modern art therapy, however, concentrates on helping those whose problems are too deep or too confused to be recognised and handled in speech, or through their normal social and family life, to deal with them through the medium of art. Artists have probably always done this to a greater or lesser extent. Goya, for example, in his Horrors of War *seems to be relieving his own soul of horrible memories as well as warning his audience of what happens when mankind becomes torturer or victim in war. Few have Goya's artistic ability but ordinary people also produce pictures laden with emotions that threaten to overwhelm them.*

Traditionally art therapy has been used in hospitals, clinics and schools for the emotionally disturbed. Now art therapists have extended their field to many other human services, particularly rehabilitation, whether in prison, hospitals or schools. Children have always been recognised as appropriate patients for art therapy and Cambodian child survivors are among those whose war trauma has been helped in this way. Art therapy has provided a way of helping those who cross cultural boundaries.

The growing interest in personal development workshops has allowed many people to use art therapy to explore their potential and make life direction decisions.

Personality

With a talent for art, the Art Therapist needs to combine robustness and sensitivity. It usually seems to be assumed that painting will be the preferred medium, but somebody with a graphic talent or a talent for modelling would be equally appropriate. Indeed a very hands on medium such as clay could well offer great opportunities for expression of primitive feelings.

Education

Candidates should have taken a degree in art. The idea that art therapy is merely 'letting them mess about with paint' and that therefore anyone can be put in charge of it is quite mistaken. Counselling and communication skills and psychotherapy training are all useful. Consult the tutors of the chosen art therapy course who may have valuable ideas about which extra external courses are most likely to be useful to you.

Access

Requirements vary, so get brochures from all the possible courses and see which is the nearest fit to your existing qualifications. Also the colleges have different slants on the subject and any personal contact you can make with staff and former students will give you important information on which will be most suited to your needs.

Candidates are usually selected for training by interview. Tutors will be looking for people who are observant of detail and can learn to interpret it and who are willing to take part in the group process rather than sit back and observe.

Career development

Most Art Therapists are driven by their interest in people with particular problems and will often have found their jobs through their contacts and reading about that problem. For instance, if you are particularly interested in traumatised children, it is likely that you will be mixing with people similarly involved and work will come through these contacts. However the professional organisation through which employment opportunities may be found is: British Association of Art Therapists, 11A Richmond Road, Brighton, Sussex BN2 3RL. It publishes a journal called *Inscape*; the subscription for individuals is £7 per copy.

Training courses are available as follows:
● University of Sheffield, Floor O, Department of Psychiatry, Art Therapy Training Programme, The Royal Hallamshire Hospital, Glossop Road, Sheffield S10 2JF. Advanced Diploma planned. Masters' degree began in September, 1990.
● Hertfordshire College of Art and Design, 7 Hatfield Road, St Albans, Hertfordshire.
Postgraduate Diploma (CNAA) in Art Therapy: Full-time one year or part-time two year course orientated to work

with the mentally ill and handicapped in the National Health Service or social services. The Diploma is approved by the Department of Health and Social Security MA in Art Therapy: Validated by CNAA. Can be continued into two year part-time MA.

● University of London, Goldsmiths' College Art Therapy Unit, 27 Albury St., Deptford, London SE8.

Post-graduate and post experience training in Art Therapy for one year full time or two years half time. *Mode 1*, Clinical, for those wishing to work in health and social services. *Mode 2*, Educational, for those wishing to work in the educational services. Study can be pursued to MPhil and PhD level.

Working conditions

The settings in which art therapy can be pursued vary widely. Prisons, mental hospitals and schools for children with special needs are only some of the places where art therapy is used. The art therapist is always in the rather unusual and inspiring position of being slightly different from all the other staff and offering the inmates or group a chance to open out and grow. With the art therapist much that has been deeply buried and too terrible to examine can be brought to light in a protected environment. Some artists say that their own work has deepened and benefited from the experiences they have had with their patients. For many people art therapy will not be a full time practice but an adjunct to a job as an art teacher or to their career as an artist. In this it is like other types of artistic work in that although you may be employed by an education or health authority, for instance, you can also be an independent professional with a number of strings to your bow.

Check List

● Is your own emotional and family life robust enough to let you maintain your own stability among people who are disturbed mentally and emotionally?
● Can your own artistic work benefit from your therapy work or, again, will you find it too emotionally demanding and bruising. Try to make contact with other art

therapists through the training courses and through your professional colleagues so as to come to a realistic assessment about this.

- To what extent is the course you have in mind tied to one particular problem, for instance, working with disturbed children? Bear in mind that your interests may change and check the possibilities of adapting what you are going to learn to other settings.
- Are you going to need the visual stimulus of new places and people for your own work? Check with the college and with your personal contacts to make sure you will be offered the opportunity to add supplementary training in particular specialisms as you need it.
- Do the people you will be working with seem to be your sort of people? Will you over a two year period find the differences stimulating or oppressive?
- Has the training organisation applied for validation, or is the diploma accredited by a professional body or learned institute other than itself?

Career planning factors

Advantageous
Art therapy has proved its worth in many situations where other approaches have failed, so the practitioner is likely to be breaking new ground and has the excitement of using his intelligence and skill to make bridges for his patients to allow them to move from their prisons of unhappiness.

Often chance social or professional contacts rather than standard career tracks will lead to an opportunity to introduce art therapy to new groups of sufferers.

The long training and the possibilities for part-time work make the subject one that can suit the timetable of a married woman who may have had to change her career plans to cater for the needs of family life.

Disadvantageous
The same factors that are viewed by one person as advantages can be stumbling blocks for a different personality.

Finance

Discretionary grants are available from some local authorities for professional courses, particularly where the candidate has the backing of a relevant respected local body or national organisation, but you will be dependent on the amount of money available at any one time and on the opinions of the grants committee. Candidates who already have a degree or professional training may be felt to have used up their entitlement to public support. Applications showing the desired training as a logical and necessary career step are most likely to be favourably received. Obtain a place on a course before making application.

Useful address

British Association of Art Therapists, 11A Richmond Road, Brighton, Sussex BN2 3RL

Books

Feldman, E.B., 1970, *Becoming Human through Art*, Prentice Hall, New Jersey.

Wadeson, Durkin and Perarch, 1989, *Advances in Art Therapy*, Wiley Interscience, Chichester.

Inscape, published by British Association of Art Therapists, subscription for individuals £7 per copy.

See also
Music Therapy, **Dance Therapy**

Ayurveda

Ayurveda is the ancient Indian system of medicine. While the name refers only to the teachings of Hinduism, the same body of ideas has contributed to one strand of Islamic medical practice in the subcontinent. In India it is possible to start from a common basic training and specialise in three main types of medicine, Western, Homoeopathic and Ayurvedic.

Personality

In this country people come to have an interest in Ayurvedic medicine for different reasons: some because they have a family background in Indian culture, others as a natural development arising from an appreciation of the Indian spiritual and artistic heritage, others again because they have been trained in the traditional skills in India and wish to continue their practice among their co-religionists.

Education

It is possible to attend lectures and demonstrations of Ayurvedic techniques in this country, but these are mainly intended for people interested from a cultural point of view or for people already in practice following training in India.

Access

Practitioners who have trained in India should contact Ayurveda Bhavan for information about their prospects of work in this country. Those who wish to take a full training in the subject should again contact either Ayurveda Bhavan or the Cultural Attache's desk at the Indian Embassy for details of courses available in India. Those starting with A level human sciences will need to complete the whole course. Exemptions will be available for those starting with medical or paramedical qualifications.

Career development

Most opportunities for practice in this country lie among the immigrant population of London, Yorkshire and the

Midlands where there are a number of thriving practices. However, interest among the population in general was raised by reports that Mrs Thatcher owed her energy to the help of an Ayurvedic practitioner.

It is not likely at present that the system will be generally available from Western doctors working under the National Health Service. It will probably therefore only be possible for doctors to make a career in this type of work in private practice. For non medically trained people career openings are probably also limited as the main ethnic group that would be likely to supply patients would tend to seek practitioners from among their own community.

Working conditions

Geographically limited as indicated above. Usually private practice and, in this country, outside the orthodox medical sphere, though accepted on equal footing in India and particularly popular among orthodox Hindus for the maintenance of health.

CHECK LIST

- Have you the cultural knowledge and linguistic skills to tackle a subject that will be taught in a strange language and against a foreign cultural background?
- Can you cope with a type of practice where there will be little professional support?
- If your interest is persistent enough to take you through the course, are there other ways than practice that you can use what you have learned, such as writing a book to explain it to others?

Career planning factors

Advantageous
Widespread public interest in things Indian and the possibility of combining training with travel. Widespread interest in interrelationship of health care systems with cultural and religious traditions.

Disadvantageous

Difficulty of attracting patients in this country if you are not a member of the Hindu community. Difficulty of gaining access to professional training both geographically and linguistically.

Finance

Unlikely to be viewed as a viable practical career by grant or loan giving bodies, although there is the possibility of approaching the subject via academic study and presenting the training as a research project.

Useful addresses

Ayurveda Bhavan, c/o Dr Ashwin Barot, 7 Ravenscroft Avenue, London NW112 0SA   081–455–39090

School of Oriental and African Studies, University of London, Malet Street, London WC1   071–637–2388

See also
Unani-Tibb

The Bates Method of Eyesight Training

Dr William Bates, a New York doctor, developed a method of training his patients to become conscious of the action of the muscles that control the focus of the eye. He believed that much poor sight was due to muscular tensions in patients under stress and that his training could bring about improvement. He therefore taught a system of relaxation and right use of the eyes which has much in common with the **Alexander Technique** *(see page 28).*

Unfortunately for Dr Bates and for his teaching, his views were distorted by followers who advocated types of exercise that were often potentially dangerous. This led to a period during which the whole system was discredited and it was difficult to find genuine instruction in the system for patients or for trainers.

As with other techniques such as Autogenic Training, **Relaxation,** Bioenergetics, **Rolfing**, *other forms of* Bodywork *and* Biofeedback, *there is in the Bates method a strong assumption that past emotional experiences have contributed to muscular tension and that when this is released material buried in the memory will come to the surface. Practitioners are trained to help their pupils cope with this experience and release themselves from past habits and prohibitions that are felt to have prevented them seeing as well as they might.*

Personality

A calm, mature personality who can convey reassurance to the patient while helping him to relax habits of lifetime tension is most desirable.

Education

Training will include the basic physics of sight, but a scientific background at least to A level and a grasp of elementary mathematics will be a help.

Access

Candidates are usually selected for training by interview during which a combination of educational background and personality will be assessed.

Career development

The present trend towards self-help in health matters has revived interest in Bates' ideas after a period of decline, caused partly by the misrepresentations noted above and partly by the apparent promise of improved technology. There have, indeed, been great advances for example in the design of contact lenses and in surgery, but there have also been considerable disadvantages and disappointments. Moreover many people would prefer to exhaust the possibilities of natural means of self-help before committing themselves to other means, particularly if they are irreversible. The Bates Association has been reorganised and a new training course leading to a diploma is being designed under its auspices based on the genuine methods of the founder. This should dispel the confusion caused by a variety of other teachings which are mistakenly attributed to Bates and make it easier to identify properly trained practitioners. There is thus a prospect of an increase in the work available. Nevertheless practice building is likely to be slow at first until the misconceptions of the past have been dispelled and more realistic estimates can be made of what can be achieved.

Working conditions

Bates practitioners need at least a 20 foot sight line for their classes, so this will usually mean hiring a classroom or hall with enough clear space. It should be possible to black out the room or have normal day light, so the curtains and windows of any offered space should be checked.

CHECK LIST

- Have you the mental, emotional and financial stamina to take up a type of practice that is only newly being revived?
- Check that any course you are offered is accredited by the Bates Association.

Career planning factors

Advantageous
This is a very portable skill. Most of the equipment used is light in weight and small.

Disadvantageous
There may not be enough demand for Bates Training locally to support a full-time practitioner. Travelling to multiple locations loads overheads on the practice which have to be found out of fees.

There is a mistaken view, arising from works on eye exercises published in Britain and India, that the Bates Method involves straining the eyes. This would certainly be harmful, particularly, for example, to people with retinal detachment. In fact, the Bates Method is based on relaxation, but the damage that has been caused to its reputation will take a long time to dispel. Understandably, workers in other fields of eye care will need the reassurance of experience before they will feel happy to cooperate with the practice of this method.

Finance

Grants are unlikely to be available for Bates Method Training in the foreseeable future. However courses are likely to be scheduled in such a way as to allow pupils to continue in employment while they are training.

Useful address

For details and availability of treatment and training contact **The Bates Association**: c/o Peter Mansfield, Hon. Secretary, Friars Court, Tarmount Lane, Shoreham by Sea, Sussex BN43 6RQ   0273 452623

Books

Huxley, Aldous 1973, *The Art of Seeing*, Perennial Books, London.

Mansfield, Peter 1992, *The Bates Method*, Macdonald Optima, London.

See also
Alexander Technique, *Autogenic Training, Bioenergetics, Biofeedback, Feldenkrais Technique, Light Therapy*, **Nutrition**, **Relaxation**.

B e l l y   D a n c i n g

It is symptomatic of much of the misunderstanding that surrounds this form of Middle Eastern dancing that even the name by which it is generally known is wrong. The original name was the dance du vent, *dance of the wind, because of the graceful gliding swaying and fluttering movements. The* re *that turned it into the* dance du ventre, *the belly dance, was added to attract sensation seekers to a display at the 1893 Chicago World Fair.*

Belly dancing has long been a tradition, not only in the tourist haunts of the Middle East, but for private celebrations among women. As well as the artistic merit of the rhythmic movements, it has the virtue of exercising the pelvic and abdominal muscles, developing suppleness and mobility in the joints and strengthening the body without building bulky muscle. It disperses fat from areas reached by few other exercise systems, taughtens and limbers muscles, especially those used in childbirth and lovemaking. With practice belly dancers gain considerable control over their internal muscles which led to prurient interest in their sexual prowess in the nineteenth century. However it is interesting that the exercises nowadays recommended for strengthening the floor of the pelvis after childbirth are almost identical with movements used by belly dancers. After a period of publicity during the early seventies, interest in belly dancing lapsed. With the passing of the craze for aerobics, a form of exercise that seemed to require people to be super fit before they began it, there is an opportunity to develop this much more holistic type of exercise which is gentle, progressive, social and artistically satisfying. For people with the physical abilities, energy and leadership talents, opportunities exist to build up groups for relaxation, weight control and exercise.

Personality

Traditionally the *dance du vent* was a social dance performed by Middle Eastern women among themselves. On occasions of family celebration and festivals parties would get together with music and their most glamorous costume to dance for each other. One must remember that, apart from slaves and the very poor, women had hardly any opportunity for physical exercise. The dance has evolved with local variations but always particularly suited to the female physique. A sympathy with the ethnic cultural background, musicality, dancing talent, and a warm optimistic personality are all desirable characteristics for someone planning a career based on this type of dance outside the night club setting.

Access

Anyone can start to learn this form of dancing at any age, but if you wish to build a career teaching it to others and learning how to use it as an aid to health or remedially, some backgrounds are more useful than others. The top teacher working in Britain at the moment is doubly qualified as a ballerina and as a State Registered Nurse. This is an ideal combination of training and experience, including as it does the anatomical knowledge to adapt the movements to the needs of the pupils and the artistic and personality elements to make the classes a challenge and a satisfaction on the mental and emotional plane.

Career development

The possibilities depend very much on the sympathies and talents of the individual. Pupils can be any age and at any level of fitness, as this form of dancing is entirely uncompetitive and builds suppleness and physical control gradually. Possible focuses of specialisation include slimming, particularly for the desk-bound who wisely do not wish to tear their ligaments to pieces by plunging into competitive sport, pre and postnatal classes, recuperative, particularly for those recovering from illnesses, operations and injuries, and general strengthening and suppling for those who suffer from back pain.

Because there is no standard career path, you will need to be your own business manager and take your own decisions about where and how to develop new groups of pupils.

Working conditions

As gymnastic equipment is not necessary, any hall or dance studio with clear space will do at a pinch but sufficient warmth, good ventilation, changing rooms, showers if possible and a pleasant atmosphere without too much noise and distraction greatly enhance the experience for class and teacher alike. The teacher will build up a suitable collection of music and will design selections to suit each class. Electric sockets will be needed for the music system, somewhere secure to store it and probably a convenient table or set of stands on which to play it.

CHECK LIST

- Check that you have the dignity and personality to persist in a field that can be the target of nudges and winks.
- As suggested above, working contacts will be predominantly women, so you should check that this will suit you.
- Check that there are other sources of suitable male company through your family and social life.
- Check that you have the energy and persistance to further your work without the back up of a professional organisation and a fixed career structure.
- Check that you have the family support to build a career.

Career planning factors

Advantageous
No formal barriers to entry. Training can be phased to suit your own circumstances.

Expenses are small and can again be phased to suit you. A thoroughly pleasant and positive activity with opportunities to travel and make fascinating international contacts.

Disadvantageous
The potential sleaze factor. No formal qualifications available. No formal career structure available.

Finance

Once you have trained and decided that you wish to introduce others to belly dancing, you will be able to start with a comparatively small outlay, as you will probably already have begun your collection of music and costume. The main expenditure will be on publicity in suitable magazines and centres visited by women and on booking time at suitable venues. However, you will need to provide for your own living expenses while you are building up your work. If you are married it is therefore essential to have the wholehearted backing of your partner.

Useful address

For individual or class tuition.
Contact Mrs Jacqueline Chapman   0733–348479

Biorhythms

Rhythmic patterns in the affairs of human beings have been observed in many different cultures. William Fliess, friend and colleague of Freud, is credited with first formalising the description of the rhythmic changes now described as biorhythms. Currently three main sine wave patterns are recognised, corresponding to the mental, emotional and physical state of each human being. As the waves are of slightly different length, they do not move on the same track, but weave a pattern round an average level, so that at any one time a variety of combinations is possible. The use and skill lies in interpreting these patterns in the light of the life style of any particular individual or occupation.

In Japan, where the system is quite widely used in industry, the charts of individual employees are recorded and they are advised of dates when they may find that they are likely to be particularly accident-prone, whether on the physical level – perhaps finding themselves unusually clumsy – on the emotional – finding themselves prone to fluctuations of mood – or on the intellectual level – finding a difficulty in concentrating, for example. It is claimed that intelligent use of the information provided by biorhythms has saved considerable sums of money for businesses such as taxi firms which rely on their drivers remaining calm and efficient in chaotic traffic conditions. Obviously the small cost of consulting a biorhythm specialist and counselling an employee could be re-couped a thousand times over if it prevented the write-off of even one modern taxi-cab.

Individuals who use the technique to plan their lives have recorded tendencies to bouts of illness at critical points on their chart and tend to schedule activities for favourable periods.

Personality

Someone of a scientific bent who enjoys working with figures, discerning patterns in statistical material and attending to detail will be attracted to this subject. To people who prefer a more intuitive approach it will seem dry and academic.

As there are few opportunities for employment, it is necessary to be robust and self-motivated enough to be happy as a consultant making your own opportunities.

This requirement of apparently introvert and extrovert characteristics in combination may pose a problem for many people.

Education

Obviously an education that has included the use of statistical methods and mathematics is helpful, but the main mathematical tools used are not too advanced to be learned by a beginner.

Access

Informal. Anyone who can understand the concepts and is able to take instruction should be able to benefit from tuition.

Career development

Opportunities in private practice are probably limited though there are individuals who wish to use the system to monitor health problems and plan their activities. Probably the most promising field for consultants is advice to industry and other larger employers, particularly where the use of heavy machinery is involved. For someone who enjoys lecturing and presentations the world is open and the opportunities depend only on your own conviction and ability to interest others in what interests you.

There is scope for further research which will involve the compilation and analysis of detailed data.

Working conditions

These will depend on your own initiative and interests. Consultants can expect to travel to clients rather than have them come to a consulting room. This is a situation which best suits those with few family ties.

CHECK LIST

- Check whether this subject is going to interest you enough long term to be a full-time job or whether it is something that you could learn as a subsidiary activity to a job in, for example, personnel management.

- Check whether your temperament enables you to be happy working as an independent consultant.
- Check again whether this will be a long term preference or whether the glamour of independence will wear off after a time.

Career planning factors

These will largely be temperamental as indicated above, but you should also consider:

Advantageous
This is a portable skill without the need for bulky equipment. The findings apply equally well in all cultures.

In an industrial world increasingly organised on an international basis a favourable response by a firm in one country may well lead to work with other affiliated companies throughout the world.

After a first burst of enthusiasm, social psychologists seem to have less and less to contribute to the understanding of working life.

It may be that new opportunities for research in more easily calculable studies, such as biorhythms, will emerge.

Finance

Grants are unlikely, but someone who can demonstrate a sensible plan for a future career using biorhythms may well be able to attract a career development loan and a business start up allowance during the first year of practice.

Useful address

London Biorhythm Company Ltd, PO Box 413, South Kensington, London SW7 2PT.
Organises lectures, training, design and production of kits and useful charts. Can supply personalised charts on receipt of necessary information.

C h i n e s e   M e d i c i n e

Westerners are now training in the use of traditional Chinese medicine.
Dispensing can take place anywhere using traditional equipment.

*Medicine developed in China and in the Western world on parallel
but different courses. The documentation of Chinese Medicine is
believed to go back six millennia, but there are two difficulties in the
way of anyone who is not a reader of Chinese and seeks to
investigate. One is that just as in Europe Aristotle's medicine notes
were emended and updated by subsequent writers and the result still
attributed to Aristotle until the end of the seventeenth century, key
Chinese texts seem to have been compiled over many hundreds of
years. Secondly, the only widely available English translation of*
The Yellow Emperor's Classic *is an English translation from a
German translation. The possibilities of confusion are obvious.*

*There are, of course, many parallels in the ideas and practice of
the two systems. However, one might say that the Chinese were
accustomed to think in terms of syndromes while the West was still
concentrating on individual signs and symptoms. In fact this tends*

to be the main reproach levelled at the Western approach. The Chinese developed a technique and vocabulary for describing their findings in terms of the balance of energy in the patient's system, dampness or dryness, heat or cold and so on.

Personality

Those who decide to study with a native Chinese should decide whether they have the patience and persistence to accept a teaching style that may be unfamiliar and uncongenial to them. Westerners are accustomed to a lively and supportive teaching style where questions are encouraged and pupils are given reasons for each step. Traditional Oriental teachers may seem authoritarian and can often impose repeated practice of detailed skills on which the pupil is expected to reflect without question. Explanations may be supplied later. Traditionally the pupil served his master during his training and counted this as a privilege.

Westerners who teach Chinese medicine may not go to these extremes in passing on their learning, but there will still be a need for what may seem a great deal of learning very dry material by heart. Moreover, if, as is only reasonable, the pupils wish to learn Chinese ideograms to improve their access to the subject, this, again, is a demanding study in terms both of character and intellect.

Education

Those who choose to learn their Chinese medicine from a Western style college will probably need to have a degree level education or at least two science A levels. A gift for languages or for the sort of philosophic approach that is able to distinguish between philosophic concepts and the words in which they are expressed in different cultures would be very helpful.

Access

A native Chinese teacher will probably not demand any formal qualifications but make his own assessment of the willingness of the pupil to learn and his suitability for the traditional pupil role. Choosing an individual master is difficult as medical skills and knowledge were often passed down in families and the trainees gradually brought into practice as they became competent in a range of skills. Their skills were not, therefore, recognised by formal diplomas. Nowadays Chinese teaching hospitals have parallel Western and Chinese medical courses and a number of Western and Australian colleges have standing arrangements to bring their students over to these as part of their training.

Career development

Chinese medicine offers a pharmacopoeia (mainly herbal and mineral), manipulative skills and the system usually referred to as acupuncture, though actually finger pressure, instruments, moxibustion and most recently, electrical probes, are used as well as needles. Although students should become generally familiar with all of these specialities, it is natural that they should have a leaning to one or the other and eventually specialise.

Chinese trained specialists can now be registered in a division of the British Register of Complementary Practitioners.

Working conditions

These will generally be those of private practice, but the considerable medical interest in Chinese medicine, both herbal and acupuncture based, suggests that there may be some openings for those trained in Chinese techniques to work with doctors or even within the Health Service. The difficulty for practitioners in this situation is that unless they are themselves Western-trained doctors as well as Chinese medicine practitioners, they are likely to find that patients are handed over to them for reasons that are not necessarily appropriate within the Chinese system. This tends to lead to what is called cookbook practice, that is, a mechanical administration of treatment, and is unlikely to be satisfying for either patient or practitioner.

CHECK LIST
_____

- Check that any course offered to you has links with a Chinese teaching hospital.
- If you intend to take a Chinese master be honest in assessing your strength of purpose and your vulnerability to the effects of culture clash.
- To get to grips with the concepts you will eventually need to learn some Chinese words and characters. Have you the linguistic skills and the turn for abstract thought that make this challenge a pleasure?

_____

Career planning factors

Any career that crosses the boundaries between two great civilisations demands both persistence and flexibility from the practitioner. It may be necessary to move between courses or colleges or countries in order to accumulate the skills you need. Australia, in keeping with its role as a Pacific power, has a well developed Chinese medical profession and it may be there that we shall see the flowering of the Chinese tradition alongside the Western tradition. Anyone interested in the subject should foster Australian contacts and watch developments there.

Increasingly various agencies are bringing in parties of Chinese medical practitioners under the auspices of the Chinese Trade Mission. It is foreseeable that this will lead to the official establishment of recognised standards of practice and qualification.

Finance

The normal considerations concerning the availability or otherwise of educational grants apply. Peculiar to the study of Chinese medicine is the likely need to travel to a Chinese teaching hospital. However the actual transport is likely to be the most expensive part of the expedition, as tuition and subsistence are, and are likely to remain for the foreseeable future, modestly priced.

Useful addresses

Academy of Chinese Acupuncture, 15–17 Southend Road, London NW3   071–794–0848

International College of Oriental Medicine, Green Hedges House, Green Hedges Avenue, East Grinstead, Sussex RH19 1DZ   0342–313106/7
Linked with International Register of Oriental Medicine.

London School of Acupuncture and Traditional Chinese Medicine, 3rd Floor, 36 Featherstone Street, London EC1Y 6QX   071–490–0513
Linked with Register of Traditional Chinese Medicine.

Each of these takes a slightly different view of the relationship between the Chinese and the Western views of medicine. Some are interested only in acupuncture as a tool, others teach it within the framework of the Chinese medical theory and others again do this but relate it to the Western view. It is important to make personal contact and understand where the college of your choice stands on these matters to avoid disappointment with your course.

Books

Ewald, Dr Hans 1978, *Acupressure Techniques*, Thorsons, London.

Veith, I., trans. 1986, *The Yellow Emperor's Classic of Internal Medicine* (*Nei Ching*), University of California Press.

Needham, J. & Gwei-Djen, L. 1980, *Celestial Lancets: A History and Rationale of Acupuncture and Moxa*, Cambridge University Press.

Kapchuk, T. 1984, *The Web that Has No Weaver*, Hutchinson, London.

See also
Acupuncture, **Reflexology**, **Shiatsu**, *Zone Therapy*

Chiropractic

Chiropractic practitioners relieve a range of back pains and other ills by specific spinal adjustments. This is one of the range of natural therapies that depend upon the manual skills of the practitioner.

Chiropractic is widely accepted by the public and by doctors as a successful way of relieving back pain, one of the main causes of lost days to industry. Less well known is the wide range of other problems that have been helped in this way as the mechanism by which improvement happens is often obscure. From the early beginnings of chiropractic, it has been asserted that almost every illness can be traced to a problem with the spinal column or the nerves that branch out from it.

Personality

Chiropractic demands a combination of academic ability to absorb scientific material, manual coordination, independence of judgement and pleasure in working with people. The temperament needed for this combination of theoretical and practical skills and type of practice resembles that of the engineer.

The chiropractor assesses his patient's state by methods that may include X-Rays if necessary, devises a suitable treatment and carries it out. Great physical strength is not needed, but someone suffering from serious disablement or deformity of the limbs or spine would be unlikely to be able to cope.

Education

School leavers need at least two science A levels in order to be able to tackle the material contained in the degree course. Mature entrants may sometimes be able to use equivalent experience gained in their previous employment, but should consult the Anglo-European College (AECC) about this. They may be recommended to take one of the access courses now starting up in colleges of further education or given specific recommendations as to what is needed to top up their knowledge in particular subjects.

Access

Candidates who can offer the necessary academic background will be further selected by interview. Tutors will be looking for people who are academically able but have an energetic and practical bent combined with powers of observation and reasoning.

Career development

The Anglo-European College of Chiropractice course takes four years full time and leads to a CNAA Degree of Bachelor of Science. After graduation the young chiropractor will work as an assistant to an experienced senior until he is ready to set up his own independent practice. It is important to find the right choice of senior and as a wise student you will begin to think about this next career step during training. The quality and variety of the experience and further training that you receive, as well as the prosperity of the practice, will have the strongest influence on your future chances of success.

A glance at the register of the British Chiropractic Association will show that practitioners are distributed in marked clusters in certain parts of the country. This is partly for a reason that applies to all the natural therapies. If an excellent practitioner comes to a new area where such services have not been available before, he may find it a slow business to build up a practice, but once his worth has become known by word of mouth the demand increases steadily. Peter Davies, PhD (*Survey of Trends in Complementary Medicine*, 1984, Institute for Complementary Medicine, London), found that for established practitioners patient/hours increased at 15 percent per year, that is doubled in five years. A study recently carried out at Sheffield University for the British Medical Association did not ask precisely the same questions but seems to have discovered similar trends in practice growth. This means that once a practice has surmounted the first difficulties of acceptance natural growth will mean that there will soon be enough demand for more practitioners to come to the area.

The largest cluster in the country is in Devon and Dorset, but this is explained by the presence of the Anglo-European

College in Boscombe. The tutors at the College also practise in the surrounding towns and villages, so that their names or those of their pupils appear in many clinics within a comfortable drive.

Some years ago chiropractic was regarded as a predominantly male profession. This is no longer so. A glance down the membership list of the British Chiropractic Association shows that the sexes are evening out. There now seem to be a number of married couples who are both chiropractors and work together in the same practice. From the point of view of allowing the wife to continue her career on a part-time basis and combine it with family responsibilities, this arrangement offers a flexibility available in few other professions. However, without wishing to be pessimistic, couples should be aware of the strains involved in sharing working and leisure time with one person and the totality of the loss involved if anything goes wrong with the relationship in either sphere.

Working conditions

Chiropractors at the beginning of their careers need to find an assistantship with an established practitioner and the possibilities open to them will dictate many of the details of their working life. They may find during their pupillage and the early years of their own private practice that they need to work in several different locations, especially if they are in a rural area where potential patients, particularly the more elderly, may otherwise find that travel difficulties make it impossible to get to a clinic.

Many practitioners find that a good pattern of work for them is to do one or two days in London or some other large conurbation and divide the rest of their time between their home base and neighbouring rural centres. Of course the overheads of town centre practices are likely to be high and these must be reflected in the scale of charges in force in the town practice. On the other hand, the patients attending these clinics may well have opportunities for high earning open to them that make this relatively unimportant to them.

The chiropractor needs to take these factors into account when planning his work and canvass the advice of established members of his Association. He should also bear in mind the considerations outlined in the section on **Counselling**, balancing his own needs for privacy and for convenience as well as the possible impact of local planning and environmental considerations.

For many practitioners the flexibility and convenience of sessional hiring in a professional practice suite has much to offer.

Check List

- Have you the necessary academic background to take on this demanding course?
- If you are at the stage of coming up to A levels write to the Anglo-European College and check that the subjects you are taking and the grades you expect to achieve are within the acceptable range.
- If you need to top up your mathematical or scientific skills, check with the staff of the Anglo-European College who are skilled in assessing the investment in time and effort needed to make up the deficit.
- Check honestly your level of motivation. Will it keep you going through a top up course and then a four year training course?
- Are you tied for emotional or other reasons to one particular area of the country? Check whether there are already practitioners working there and find out from them how they assess professional prospects.
- If your preferred area has not yet been opened up, have you the persistence, self-confidence and financial backing to be a pioneer, knowing that the next generation of practitioners may be the major beneficiaries of your efforts?
- Check with the tutorial staff of the Anglo-European College if you do not know any former students who can give you a retrospective view of the course and a realistic picture of day to day working conditions.

Career planning factors

Advantageous
The training for this career leads to the award of a degree.

This fact does not mean that you are better than any of the many excellent chiropractors who were trained in former years, but it gives you recognition in the outside world for the standard of work that you have achieved.

If this is the first degree course that you have enrolled for, you should be able to claim a grant for your studies from your Local Education Authority.

The AECC has set itself a programme of research with a view to providing a scientific underpinning of its work. Students and graduates of the College are encouraged to participate in this and to extend the scope of their ideas and studies.

Disadvantageous

Chiropractic is the type of therapy that has in the past had the reputation for accepting most wholeheartedly the views of the medical profession. You must decide whether this is for you an advantage or a disadvantage. It is the proclaimed wish of the AECC to stimulate research and scientific enquiry, so as younger members of the profession feed through into senior posts one may expect to see change in the direction of increased openness.

Finance

Local Education Authority grants available. Obtain a place on the course before making application.

Useful address

Anglo-European College of Chiropractic, 13–15 Parkwood Road, Boscombe, Bournemouth, Dorset BH5 2DF   0202–431021
Graduates of the AECC are eligible to become members of the British Chiropractic Association.

Book

Michael Copland-Griffiths, DC, *Dynamic Chiropractic Today*, Thorsons, London.

See also
Manipulation, **Osteopathy**

Clinic Management

To mention clinic management as a career worth engaging in for its own sake is to have the older generation of practitioner snorting with annoyance. 'I never needed to do any managing,' they grumble, or alternatively: 'Far too much talk about all this sort of thing, in my day you just went ahead and managed.'

It is true that in the past many very successful practices have been built on common sense and excellent therapeutic technique. However many of these were built up when life was very much simpler. Nowadays many of the training colleges and courses incorporate a module on practice management within their course and this is quite right, as practice management is one of the competences that the successful practitioner needs. However, as we have mentioned in many of the entries in this book, there is a tendency to move away from the single practitioner clinic, even away from the single type of practice clinic towards the larger professional multi-skill clinic. This means that the many services and facilities that the practitioner needs are professionally provided so that the practitioner is able to concentrate on the essential business of looking after the patient.

Personality

A warm and energetic personality capable of self discipline and of demanding it from others is essential for success in this field. The manager or owner of a professional clinic is rather in the position of a pub landlord. Harmony between the people involved and high standards of behaviour are essential for success. The manager needs the personality to bring strong-willed and idiosyncratic people together and the business sense to make sure that all their practices flourish. His clinic depends on their success.

Education

There are a number of possible ways of becoming a clinic manager. Obviously an interest in the complementary therapies and a knowledge of what they can offer to patients is necessary but it does not have to be a detailed knowledge, though some practitioners have gone on to become excellent clinic managers.

Essentially the business side can be seen as the letting of specialised space. Therefore a variety of different types of business training could provide useful skills. Book-keeping and accountancy, building management, hotel and conference management, personnel management are all possible types of background.

Apart from these formal skills, experience in running the business side of a clinic would be extremely useful. Ideally it would be most pleasant to work in a really well-run clinic for a short period but realistically it is true to say that one can often learn most from a bad example. For a conscientious person it is always worrying to see things being done badly but many useful lessons can be learned from the analysis of mistakes and one should not refuse the offer of a temporary position merely because the clinic is suspected not to be of the very best.

Access

If you wish to be employed as a manager by someone who is investing in a set of practice rooms, you will need to have made your name in a related field. You will then depend on the chance that there may be someone with funds to invest and the chance that you are able to meet that person through the press or through personal contacts and are then able to convince him that he should hire you to manage his investment. You may think that this scenario depends to far too great a degree on chance and this is quite correct. You may also reflect that your salary will come out of the profits of the building but that those profits will belong to the owner of the business, although you will have put your time and energy into building it up.

You may therefore consider that a more realistic plan is to run your own clinic. This is a considerable step from a personal and a financial point of view. We raise below points that you should consider both before and after making the decision that this is what you want to do.

Career development

The early months of your career running a complementary health clinic are likely to be extremely hard going. Anyone who has been involved in refurbishing a building will know how easy it is for deadlines to slip behind and how easily unforeseen extras can mount up.

The secret both before opening and when the clinic is running lies in planning and quality control. Every possible disaster has to be foreseen, the response planned if it is going to be unavoidable and the disaster if possible forestalled. Quality is easier to control than it has ever been with the setting of standards for practitioners. As sections open for the different types of practice on the British Register it is possible to know exactly what the practitioners with whom you are working can be expected to deliver and they can each know that they can talk on terms of mutual respect to colleagues who have full competence in their own fields.

When you have attracted a list of practitioners who are all of the highest standards themselves and know that their neighbours in the building are the same you have the basis of a harmonious and prosperous clinic. Then, rather than resting on your laurels you need to be thinking how to develop what you have built up. Should you enlarge your current facility, open it more hours a day, so as to make more use of existing assets, or set up another on the same plan elsewhere?

A useful development path for many young businesses is to franchise their own scheme to other entrepreneurs. This tends to work particularly well with retail outlets, but could pose considerable problems for anyone working in the field of health maintenance. The problem of controlling the standards maintained by franchisees is much more difficult in this field. Unfortunately also a number of franchising, multiple level marketing and pyramid selling organisations from the United States of America have dented public confidence in these forms of business expansion, especially as applied to health products and services.

Whether you can reproduce your original success and set up, by whatever means, a chain of clinics will depend on your skill in selecting suitable people to become managers for you and in developing procedures, training practices and relations with the public.

Working conditions

At the beginning, however well financed you may be, you are likely to find yourself doing every job in the house, from janitor to managing director and this is of inestimable benefit because it is the details, such as waste disposal for example, that an outsider might overlook as trivial that reveal whether or not the whole concern is running smoothly. During your learning time you will come to know where to look to judge the efficiency of a clinic team and how the figures in the books reflect their activities. This knowledge will be invaluable when you are at a stage of working predominantly on the purely managerial plane.

CHECK LIST

- Far too many ventures have foundered because they have been started with high ideals but too little practical expertise. Check carefully what technical advice is available to you. You will need to be able to count on the services of:
  - a financial adviser,
  - a solicitor, and
  - an insurance broker
  - at the least.
- Check that your advisers are of the kind appropriate to your situation. For example, do not insist that your solicitor who is an old family friend advises you on business matters. These might be better handled by a specialist in commercial matters. Very often the best advice a professional adviser can give you is to refer you to the right expert for a particular job.
- Check the level of risk that you can feel happy with. For example many people are encouraged to use their homes as security for loans to start a business.

Colour Therapy

It has been recognised at many different times and places that people are affected by the colours that surround them and that they express a great deal about their feelings and character by their choice of colour. This has been connected in ancient times, and still is in some cultures, with astrology, numerology and alchemy.

In modern times the phenomena have been studied from a variety of more scientific perspectives. On the most pedestrian level one can find colour consultants who advise on suitable colours for make-up and clothing. This may seem trivial, but can contribute to self-confidence and thus success in work and private life as well as to a general sensation of wellbeing.

A more sophisticated application is advising individuals and firms and institutions on suitable colours for their buildings and furniture. This involves taking care that the effect of colour on mood and health as well as the aesthetic aspects are taken into account.

Trials have shown that it is possible to make measurable physical differences by the effect of light alone, for example, to lower the blood pressure of a group of people by showing them cool colours and raise it by showing hot colours. Similarly the effectiveness of full spectrum light in relieving Seasonal Affective Disease (the depression suffered by some people during the dark winter months) is widely recognised by the medical profession.

Some practitioners specialise in the use of coloured light directly applied to patients in specific patterns in order to help make differences of this kind. Others, who more often refer to themselves as colour healers, as well as giving patients the experience of the colours, instruct the patients to meditate on the colours or to imagine themselves breathing them. So powerful is the effect of the mind on the body and vice versa that patients report significant speeding up of their recovery and benefits in terms of mental and emotional peace and stability.

Personality

People are usually attracted to colour therapy in the first place from artistic motives. However, some of the most successful practitioners combine with their artistic sensitivity a scientific approach and a deep interest in the theoretical underpinning of the physical phenomena with which they work.

Education

Most training courses give at least a framework of information describing light and how it is seen as colour when it impinges on certain pigments or when fractions of its spectrum are screened out. However, all this will come much more easily to those who have a background in physics and are accustomed to the idea of light waves as merely one type of energy radiating in the universe than to those who have only thought of colour as paint applied to surfaces.

Access

Generally informal. Most courses are based on weekend workshops and so are accessible to those who need to earn while they learn.

Career development

Training courses are predominantly part time. It is possible to register with the British Register of Complementary Practitioners (Colour Therapy Division). The subject is only gradually being formalised, so that from the career point of view the advantages of easy access and no rigid requirements of previous learning are counterbalanced by the lack of a well marked career path.

There is a tendency among organisations to be willing to use a colour therapist as adviser on decoration of buildings, because they can see that they are getting something for their money. These clients, however, often fail to reflect that providing soothing decoration for disturbed children, without giving them the follow up of training to internalise the effects of the colours is little better than giving them a tranquiliser. The practitioner who succeeds in convincing his client that colour therapy is not just about externals but a way of giving a message to the whole patient at a very deep level will have the best chance of helping effectively. So far the group that have gone farthest in this direction are probably the followers of Rudolf Steiner, largely because of their wealth of experience in looking after disturbed children and retarded children and adults.

Working conditions

Obviously these will vary according to the field in which the practitioner chooses to work.

Colour healers will receive individual patients in a practice room in the normal way and will probably find it most convenient to work at home or somewhere where they can rig up lighting apparatus safely and conveniently without having to dismount it between sessions. This obviously implies a certain investment in premises and equipment.

Those whose work is predominantly in an institutional setting, children's homes, prisons, schools or colleges, will need to arrange their equipment in easily portable modules and to invest in a van or some other form of transport sturdy and secure enough to be used for storage when not actually on the road.

CHECK LIST

- Check the widest variety of brochures offering courses to make sure which are most appropriate to the sort of work that you would prefer.
- Check to make sure what assumptions the organisers make about your previous learning and experience. It is always a good idea to ring up and ask if you can go and talk to the organiser of a course before signing up so as to avoid misunderstandings later.

Career planning factors

The commercial side of the work, which is probably the least satisfying to the dedicated practitioner is probably the most stable in terms of offering a career. However for someone who can start to work part time, perhaps combining it with family life, practice in the healing side may be very rewarding in terms of personal satisfaction and slowly build up to a useful financial contribution as well.

Finance

This subject is unlikely to attract an educational grant but you may well be able to interest your local Training and

Enterprise Council (TEC) in backing you for a career development loan or other arrangements that they are administering locally.

Useful addresses

British Register of Complementary Practitioners (Colour Therapy Section), c/o The Institute for Complementary Medicine

Hygeia Studios, Brook House, Avening, Tetbury, Gloucestershire GL8 8NS   Nailsworth 2150
Contact: Theo Gimbel.

International Association of Colour Healers, 67 Farm Crescent, Wexham Court, Slough, Berkshire SL2 5TQ   0753–76913
Contact: Mrs Jan Davidson.

International Association of Colour Therapists, Endellion, Money Row Green, Holyport, Maidenhead, Berkshire SL6 2HA   0628–34777

Living Colour, 33 Lancaster Grove, London NW3 4EX   071–794–1371

Books

Babitt, Edwin 1878, *Principles of Light and Colour*, Citadel.

Birren, Faber 1969, *Light, Colour and Environment*, Van Nostrand, New York.

Birren, Faber 1978, *Color and Human Response*, Van Nostrand, New York.

Luscher, Dr Max 1987, *The Luscher Colour Test*, Various translations, Pan Books, London.

See also
Aromatherapy, Healing

Counselling

Counsellors may develop specialities such as Assertiveness Training for clients whose lives are being ruined by their own lack of self-confidence.

Counselling has been described as the art of listening constructively. Most counsellors claim to be non-directive, that is they do not aim to influence their clients to act in a particular way but to help them explore their situation and the options open to them and then make their own decisions. In fact inevitably there will be some influence but within the discipline the degree, context and desirability of such influence are all live issues.

Within the discipline there are also different understandings of the psychological theory underpinning the practice. Counselling is considered appropriate to clients dealing with difficult life situations and emotional problems, not to people with severe mental illness.

Counselling is undertaken by many different practitioners, both in the course of practising other disciplines and as a practice on its own. If you are contemplating taking a course in the subject, it is wise to consider how you want to use it.

For those who want to counsel as a profession in itself, there are many training courses available, through universities, polytechnics, private training courses, courses mounted by groups of various religious or doctrinal affiliation and various individual teachers. They are usually about two years long, leading to a diploma, or one year leading to a certificate. Expect to devote one weekend a month or one day a week to tutorial sessions and a considerable amount of thought and time to homework.

Short courses in counselling skills are also available from many of the same sources. These usually amount to a week's summer school or a succession of three weekends. They are not a qualification to practise but can be a useful introduction to the sort of skills involved. Counselling skills can be used to improve effective communication in industry, medicine and complementary medical practice and many other settings. Counselling skills modules are now incorporated in training courses for many different professions. Short skill courses are also a useful way of dipping a toe in the water for someone who is not yet sure whether to make the commitment to a long and expensive professional training course.

Personality

A mature personality who knows from experience the pains and joys of life has most to offer. This is a profession that can lead to burn-out, so sensitivity needs to be supported by emotional robustness. Counsellors may need to be strong in order to prevent a session running off the track but must not let their own personality intrude. Anyone with even mild exhibitionist tendencies would feel frustrated.

Education

Most people undertaking training, but by no means all, start with a degree nowadays. A psychology degree may be helpful, but successful counsellors have come from many different backgrounds. More important than any particular subject is the ability to digest and learn from life experience. Many counselling training courses are described as experiential, that is they teach the trainees in the group by helping them explore their own feelings and life history. They should also teach the pupil the ideas underlying practice and needed for discussion with colleagues.

Access

Candidates are usually selected for training by interview. Tutors will be looking for people who are observant of detail and can learn to interpret it and who are willing to take part in the group process rather than sit back and observe.

Career development

Many people working as counsellors will dismiss the idea that they have a career; they see what they do as an art of vocation. However, some general patterns emerge.

Counselling is a popular choice for a second career. This is partly because people are seldom mature enough on leaving school or university.

A counsellor who wishes to maintain and improve his/her competence will regularly take part in in-service training and will have a supervision relationship. Such arrangements are mandatory in most of the professional organisations and, when fully developed, are beneficial on a number of levels.

The newly trained counsellor will arrange to be supervised by someone from the same training background, but senior to himself. Later he will move on to someone from a different background and to someone on the same level as himself; peer supervision. Finally he will supervise his juniors, a step that may lead on to undertaking the training of his successors. For the individual practitioner, this provides continued learning experience and monitors that he maintains his professional skills at the highest standard. It also provides emotional support through the opportunity for discussion with an experienced colleague in a regular and structured way.

A proper professional support system should be able to moderate and accommodate genuine innovation, while preventing innovators from declining into mere eccentricity. This is beneficial both in preventing ossification of the discipline and for strengthening professional organisations as funds and personnel resources are less likely to be dissipated by recurring fission.

There is a Counselling Section of the British Register for Complementary Practitioners and the British Association for Counselling has a category of Accredited Counsellors.

Working conditions

Counselling takes place in many different contexts: within the National Health Service and Social Services, under the auspices of voluntary bodies, such as Cruse, Relate, Samaritans, and in private practice.

In the case of the first two, the sponsoring body will lay down guidelines as to what they expect of practitioners and will provide the rooms. The quality of both management and physical space vary very much according to the personalities and priorities locally. Within the National Health Service, for example, counsellors may find rooms more depressing and clinical than they would like. They should not find that they are constantly disturbed when with clients, that their appointments are mishandled or that they have to shift sessions to a new site each time. When conditions are as unsatisfactory as this, it may be necessary to take formal steps to get matters improved.

Counsellors in private practice need to decide where they should hold sessions, bearing in mind their own need for privacy and that of the client for confidentiality. Working at home has apparent advantages of cheapness, convenience and informality, but there are disadvantages. The territory is not neutral, but belongs to one of the participants, family members may interrupt, confidentiality may be compromised, as may the counsellor's privacy. Planning and environmental aspects need to be checked with the Local Authority. A new worry is uncertainty over the possibility that the home may be assessed for the Unified Business Rate as well as the Community Charge. Many counsellors now feel that hiring a room in a professional practice suite on a sessional basis is better. In exchange for the sessional rent the provider of the service takes off the practitioner's shoulders the problems of rent, rates, cleaning and reception.

CHECK LIST

- Is the course based on one particular understanding of the psychological development of personality, or does it consider a number of different views?

- If the first, are you likely to be tied to one professional body or clique? Will you be dependent on them for clients and future professional life, or are the qualifications valid for work in other counselling settings?
- Similarly, to what extent is the course tied to one particular problem, for example marital problems? Bear in mind that your interests may change. A general course with a module about your particular interest may provide you with more future flexibility. You can then add supplementary training in particular specialisms as you need it.
- Do the people you will be working with seem to be your sort of people? Will you over a two year period find the differences stimulating or oppressive?
- Has the training organisation applied for validation, or is the diploma accredited by a professional body or learned institute other than itself?
- What resources does the training organisation make available to you – libraries – personal counselling – study rooms – different specialist staff?
- Can the tutorial staff put you in touch with former students who can give you a retrospective view of the course?
- Are there opportunities for further personal and career development?

Career planning factors

Advantageous

Much counselling takes place under the auspices of voluntary organisations. This provides opportunities for new counsellors who can afford not to take a fee to work their way in and gain professional experience. Voluntary work should not be seen as less than professional. The standard is high and rising. The selection for a place as a voluntary worker will be just as competitive and rigorous as for a salaried or fee-earning position.

Counselling is increasingly valued by GPs, by industry and the public. For example a commercial insurance company has recently written into its victim protection policies cover for one thousand pounds worth of stress counselling from members of the British Register of Complementary Practitioners (Counselling Division). This means that people like bank employees and guards who were formerly only covered for the physical results of accident and assault are now able to get timely help for the range of emotional and mental damage known as post traumatic stress syndrome.

Disadvantageous
The existence of the voluntary sector might be seen as reducing the rate of fees in the profession.

Counsellors need to be realistic about the potential effect of their work on their emotions and relationships, particularly if specialising in fields such as cancer, crisis counselling and marital breakdown. A sound career plan should build in changes of speciality, self care and continual retraining.

Finance

Discretionary grants are available from some local authorities for professional courses, particularly where the candidate has the backing of a relevant respected local body or national organisation, but you will be dependent on the amount of money available at any one time and on the opinions of the grants committee. Candidates who already have a degree or professional training may be felt to have used up their entitlement to public support. Applications showing the desired training as a logical and necessary career step are most likely to be favourably received. Obtain a place on a course before making application.

Useful addresses

The British Association for Counselling, 37A Sheep Street, Rugby CV21 3BX   0788–78328
This Association provides a forum for counsellors, lists counsellors up and down the country and notes what subjects they specialise in. It also accredits a small number of counsellors and a few of the many courses in existence.

The British Register of Complementary Practitioners has a

Counselling Division which is open for applications from individuals. The Institute for Complementary Medicine can discuss applications for registration of individual counsellors and accreditation of courses as suitable to train counsellors for registration. (See page 4 for the Institute for Complementary Medicine's address.)

Books

The subject is so wide that any book will tell only part of the story. The following are chosen for their contrasting style and views as well as for their useful contact lists and bibliographies: Sandford, Christine, and Beardsley, Wyn 1986, *Making Relationships Work*, Sheldon Press, London.

Quilliam, Susan and Grove-Stephenson, Ian 1990, *The Counselling Handbook*, Thorsons, London.

See also
Hypnotherapy, Psychotherapy

Crystal Therapy

Most civilisations have attributed special powers to gem stones. With the discovery of radio waves and the properties of crystals, on which radio technology and the modern computer industry are based, a plausible foundation for a variety of incompatible notions is gradually emerging. Crystals of various kinds are used by many different types of practitioner. The remarks below refer to one of the most structured and accessible approaches.

Personality

This type of practice appeals to people of scientific bent who are prepared to grapple with ideas still at the stage of development.

Education

Unless one is content to use the techniques blindly a basic understanding of the underlying physical phenomena is essential. However the wide availability of computers and the popular interest in electronic engineering have made it easier than it used to be for people without a formal qualification in physics to gain a general acquaintance with the field.

Access

Most practitioners who move into this field do so from a background of training in another type of therapy such as acupuncture or osteopathy. Often they have combined this with an interest in electronic engineering. A level knowledge of anatomy, physiology or a recognised diploma in these subjects and diagnostic skills are assumed.

Career development

Training in electro-crystal therapy is by a series of seven weekend workshops. As the individual units are repeated several times during a cycle of 18 months, it is possible to repeat some if necessary, or to schedule attendance flexibly to fit in with work commitments. The seven units are supported with home study and with units of supervised clinical practice.

Learning a further skill is an exciting step for any practitioner, but it needs to be carefully planned in full awareness of the implications. In the years immediately following graduation from the first training course the practitioner will probably be fully occupied building up the practice, either working with colleagues or on his or her own account. Money will probably also be short. It is important during this extremely busy period not to subject yourself to too much financial or physical strain, so as to remain at peak effectiveness for your patients and partners. Once you have built up a small financial cushion and have a working routine well established with a reliable case load, you can start thinking about investing in the future by enhancing your skills with others that complement what you can already offer. Inevitably this will draw in new, possibly different, types of patient.

Working conditions

Extra activities and equipment may require you to re-think the way your clinic is planned and the scheduling of your week.

CHECK LIST

- Check your current financial and time commitments. Can you afford to undertake further training now?
- If you introduce a new therapy at your clinic, what will be the impact on your current way of working?
- Will you need to change the arrangements you have worked out with your receptionist?
- Is it possible to run clinics for different types of therapy on the same day? In the same rooms? Should they be kept quite separate?
- Will a different physical layout be needed? More furniture?
- With the help of your accountant, monitor the cash flow pattern of your new working arrangement. Are changes needed in your billing or other working habits?

Career planning factors

Advantageous
A wider range of skills increases the interest of the work, attracts new and different types of patients, makes it possible to help more people with a better service.

Disadvantageous
The introduction of a new type of therapy needs to be managed carefully. Your professionalism will not let you make the mistake of confusing your patients about what is going on by switching between different types of therapy without explanation or permission.

Finance

A Career Development Loan may be a possibility, but you will probably not wish to burden yourself with this cost. Consult your accountant about the possibility of offsetting the cost of this further training against income tax. He should be able to persuade the tax inspector that this allowance can be justified.

Useful address

For information about cost and scheduling of courses, contact Harry Oldfield, Electro-Crystal Therapy, 117 Long Drive, South Ruislip, Middlesex HA4 0HG   081–841–1716

Books

Oldfield, H. 1987, *Electro-Crystal Therapy*, Thorsons, London.

See also
Radionics

Dance Therapy

Exploring movements with patients whose ills are emotional as well as bodily.

Dance is one of the foundation arts which exists in some form in the most primitive civilisations and has connections with the springs of music, drama and religion. At its crudest it may be seen as a thoroughly enjoyable form of exercise for the body which will also bring relaxation and refreshment to mind and spirit. However, the expression dance therapy usually refers to the psychotherapeutic benefits of dance. These are widely recognised and many different approaches have been devised appropriate to different types of patient.

Personality

The dancer who uses the art therapeutically needs to hold two apparently contradictory demands in tension. The rewards of stardom are not available in this field, but the dancer's own artistic conscience will demand that she maintain her own high standards of technique and expression while being conscious that the aim for patients is not necessarily excellence of performance but personal therapy. It takes real humility and self motivation to work in this way.

Education

A sound training in classical and/or modern dance is essential. The more this is backed up by a wide-ranging general education and experience of the richness and variety of human culture, the wider the range of sympathy and understanding the dance therapist has to offer patients.

Access

The field is changing and expanding. Dancers who think they would be interested should contact their local hospital's psychiatric department to see whether there are openings for training or gaining experience locally. A selection of addresses is given below representing some of the types of specialist training available.

Career development

Satisfaction will be found in developing excellence in your own speciality and in the esteem of colleagues and patients rather than in opportunities for promotion in a hierarchy. Someone who wishes to combine a career with family life might well find it possible to carve themselves out a niche within the social or health services of their local community that would allow the flexibility they need.

Working conditions

Dance therapists work in prisons, hospitals, schools and many other settings with people of all ages and types. Retarded children, disturbed people of all ages, geriatric patients and patients recovering from heart attacks are among those who benefit from dance therapy.

CHECK LIST

- Is your own emotional and family life robust enough to let your maintain your own stability among people who may be disturbed mentally and emotionally?
- Can your own artistic work benefit from your therapy work or, again, will you find it too emotionally demanding and bruising. Try to make contact with other dance therapists through the training courses and through your professional colleagues so as to come to a realistic assessment about this.
- To what extent is the course you have in mind tied to one particular problem, for instance, working with disturbed children? Bear in mind that your interests may change and check the possibilities of adapting what you are going to learn to other settings.
- Can your therapeutic work be combined with teaching or developing your other artistic interests? Are you going to find sufficient stimulus either in your work place or in your outside interests to maintain your freshness and energy for your patients and for your own work? Check with the college and with your personal contacts the chances of supplementing your current competence with training in particular specialisms as you need it.
- Do the people you will be working with seem to be your sort of people? Will you over a period find the differences stimulating or oppressive? Are there opportunities for movement within the institution or area where you will be working?
- Has the training organisation applied for validation, or is

the diploma accredited by a professional body or learned institute other than itself?

Career planning factors

Advantageous
Dance therapy has proved its worth in many situations where other approaches have failed, so the practitioner is likely to be breaking new ground and has the excitement of using intelligence and skill to make bridges for his patients to allow them to rediscover worlds of emotion and physical sensation that may have been closed to them since early childhood.

Often chance social or professional contacts rather than standard career tracks will lead to an opportunity to introduce dance therapy to new groups of sufferers.

The possibilities for part-time work make the subject one that can suit the timetable of a married woman who may have had to change her career plans to cater for the needs of family life.

Disadvantageous
The same factors that are viewed by one person as advantages can be stumbling blocks for a different personality. Make a realistic analysis of your needs.

Finance

Discretionary grants are available from some local authorities for professional courses, particularly where the candidate has the backing of a relevant respected local body or national organisation, but you will be dependent on the amount of money available at any one time and on the opinions of the grants committee. Candidates who already have a degree or professional training may be felt to have used up their entitlement to public support. Applications showing the desired training as a logical and necessary career step are most likely to be favourably received. People are usually given contradictory advice about whether to seek a grant or a place on a course first. On balance it is probably marginally easier to find a place on a course before making application.

Useful addresses

Hertfordshire College of Art and Design, 7 Hatfield Road, St. Albans, Hertfordshire.

Association for Dance Movement Therapy.
Write for information to Hertfordshire College, above.

Arts Therapies Department, Springfield House, Glenburney Road, Tooting Bec, London SW17 7DJ
Workshops held in London, Birmingham and Edinburgh.

Laban Art of Movement Guild, Boynnes, Hadley Common, Hertfordshire EN5 5QG   081–449–5268

Margaret Morris Movement Therapy, Suite 3/4, 39 Hope Street, Glasgow G2 6AG   041–334–1288

Medau Society, 8b Robson House, East Street, Epsom, Surrey   03727–29056

See also
Art Therapy, Belly Dancing, Music Therapy, Dramatherapy

Disability

People who may suffer a particular disability vary widely in what they can tackle. There are many who can benefit from some among the many techniques of complementary medicine and others who can well find a profession as a practitioner.

Carers who wish to learn massage, aromatherapy, reflexology or some other skill to help someone in their own family should consider whether they could not be more ambitious and take a professional training course. Of course they wish to offer the best within the family, but there is no reason why this cannot be combined with personal satisfaction and the development of a new career.

Professional social or care workers will already be accustomed to value professional qualifications and standards. They will welcome the opportunity to expand their competences into a new field of practical value to their clients.

Where there are already existing links with the disabled community these are noted under subject headings.

Education

Current debate as to whether education within the general community is really in the best interests of young people with disability is relevant here. The disabled would-be student needs to be confident that he has achieved a sound educational basis so that he can concentrate on his subject without the distraction of trying to make up gaps.

Access

Carers whose interest has only been roused in the first instance because of a family situation may find that they need to gain additional background knowledge from adult or further education courses because their change of direction was unplanned.

Disabled students may meet initial scepticism when applying for courses because tutors may never have planned for their special needs before. Teaching methods may need to be completely re-thought, or even reversed. For example, an osteopathy tutor who was accustomed to see anatomy taught separately from manipulative techniques found that for his blind students both had to be taught hands on and that after the first lessons the two subjects needed to be taught together. Using a tape recorder, he developed a system of recording each tutorial session and sending the student home with the tape to play it back and follow the movements during his practice sessions. Examination techniques may also need to be redesigned in modes suited to the possibilities of the individual student.

Career development

Both carers and the disabled themselves are likely to have access to a network of support groups and professionals concerned with people with similar problems and in this respect they may have a positive advantage over the average student setting up in practice after his training.

They also have special insights gained from practical experience that may take an outsider many years to build up.

With the development of National Vocational Qualifications in Care in the Community, it is likely that the whole situation of the disabled and their carers will become much easier to understand. It is hoped that bridging qualifications will be developed in order to allow qualified practitioners of the natural therapies to deploy their skills for the disabled and to help carers and such professionals as social workers understand the scope of the therapies and their application in this field.

As more and more sections of the British Register of Complementary Practitioners open for applications, we shall see the development of dual qualifications: social worker/practitioners and carer/practitioners. We can also expect many practitioners who started their careers from the experience of disablement, just as many complementary practitioners have always started from the experience of the effectivenss of the complementary therapies in their own case.

Working conditions

The day centres and support groups run for people with disability may well be able to provide a venue for treatment at no cost, so practitioners from whatever background may find that work in this setting can be carried out on a fee scale that would be uneconomic for other groups.

Within the foreseeable future it may become possible for treatment fees to be reimbursed from National Health Service funds. At present this is only a widely acknowledged wish and cost is seen as an obstacle, but if it is proved that treatments can help keep clients independent the very modest fees may prove to be a cost effective alternative to institutional care.

A research project is in progress to ascertain the amount of work going on among the disabled at present, its scope for development and the best ways to foster it.

CHECK LIST ─────────────────────────────────

● Using this book and other resources open to you check where your particular circumstances fit in this context.

Career planning factors

It seems amazing that the complementary therapies have not so far been much developed for and among people with a disability. The historical reasons are probably that the disabled are such a diverse community, that they are felt to belong to the National Health Service or the Social Services and that complementary practitioners who might wish to help are confused about questions of responsibility and accreditation. There is also the problem of finance. The disabled are likely by virtue of their condition to have little disposable income and would therefore be unlikely to be able to afford fees for complementary health care.

These financial constraints could disappear if the results of current studies of the usefulness of the natural therapies stimulate some allocation of funds for such treatments.

The ownership problem is already being addressed by the growing consciousness among disabled people themselves and their carers that except in the few obvious cases of certain types of mental disability the disabled own themselves and that their independence should be encouraged wherever possible.

A practical move to enfranchising these citizens and their carers would be the development of training modules, if possible recognised as qualifying units for National Vocational Qualifications, for workers with the disabled who want to add complementary therapies to their skills and for complementary therapy practitioners who want to work among people with a disability.

What must be resisted at all costs is the development of a second class service of complementary skills for the disabled. Both as patients and as practitioners disabled people should be offered access to the best service and training available, followed where appropriate by the same registration open to other people of the same competence.

Finance

As well as the normal sources of training finance, people with a disability and their carers may be able to interest special charities, interest groups or support groups in financing their training. However, lateral thinking is the key here and if you can get a group of committed people together within your local group, there is every reason to approach established training schools to see whether they will co-operate in developing suitably adapted versions of their existing courses. The training colleges are predominantly privately run charitable trusts or businesses. This means that they can be expected to respond to demand if it is presented to them as a substantial and manageable growth of their intake.

Dramatherapy

Psychotherapists have used techniques of role playing in different ways for many years. The work of Moreno is a case in point. In these cases patients were required to act what they saw as their own situation or take on the roles of other people involved in their personal drama. The logical step of using trained actors with psychotherapeutic skills to help patients arrive at an understanding of themselves, their situation and the feelings of the other people involved in it has only been taken over time and is still regarded as daring in some quarters.

Personality

As a result of their professional training actors are able to project their personalities and seem more real than other people. The actor who combines this skill with the gift of cutting to the emotional truth of a situation will be best fitted for drama therapy.

Education

A sound training in drama is needed, underpinned by a wide general education to allow you to empathise with people from the widest possible range of cultural and social backgrounds.

Access

If you decide to investigate possibilities of moving into this field, consider if there is a particular type of patient to whose problems you feel drawn, whether by personal experience or by something that you have read or heard from the media. Then start making contact, perhaps first via the information service of your local library with the psychiatric departments of local hospitals, the social services, local centres catering for people with disabilities, any prisons that there may be in your area. Contact also the British Association of Dramatherapists who may be able to tell you of developments in your own area that you would not hear of from any other source. You can get in touch with them c/o Hatfield Polytechnic, PO Box 30, Hatfield AL10 9AL.

Career development

You should aim to take a two year diploma course in the subject and to keep up to date by attending workshops and discussing your work with colleagues. There are few set career paths, so that how and in what directions you progress will depend on your own ability to convince those officially in charge of the organisations within which you work of the value of what you do. Where the management is imaginative and willing to provide the framework within which you can develop your work, this can be an immensely stimulating situation. You may find that the temptation always is to throw yourself into an almost impossible situation and undertake more and more responsibility without the institutional back up to allow the work to survive without you.

Working conditions

It would be misleading to suggest that prisons, mental hospitals and many others of the settings in which dramatherapy has much to offer are cheerful and supportive. However, the sheer goodwill of those involved in therapeutic enterprises of this kind is such that the material obstacles are often seen as a challenge to intensify effort.

People who practise a therapy of this kind are bringing their artistic and interpretative skill into a closed society from the outside world. This can be of great benefit to their patients and relieve the hopelessness engendered by the institutional setting. However, it does leave the therapists to some extent at risk in that they can be seen as marginal, a frill, and be left out of decision-making that affects them and their patients as well as all the other workers in the institution. It is therefore essential to participate in as many activities and organisations as possible so as to keep the value of your contribution before the authorities and the wider public as well as maintaining your own keenness.

Check List

- Is your own emotional and family life robust enough to let you maintain your own stability among people who may

be disturbed mentally and emotionally?
- Have you made a realistic assessment of your own emotional and physical stamina? It is wise to fix an end date for any particular enterprise at which point you will review the situation and decide whether to change your sphere of operations or fix another period during which you will continue the work.
- Can your own artistic work benefit from your therapy work or, again, will you find it too emotionally demanding and bruising? Try to make contact with other art therapists through the training courses and through your professional colleagues so as to come to a realistic assessment about this.
- To what extent is the course you have in mind tied to one particular problem, for instance, working with disturbed children? Bear in mind that your interests may change and check the possibilities of adapting what you are going to learn to other settings.
- Are you going to need the visual stimulus of new places and people for your work? Check with the college and with your personal contacts then add supplementary training in particular specialisms as you need it.
- Do the people you will be working with seem to be your sort of people? Will you over a two year period find the differences stimulating or oppressive?
- Has the training organisation applied for validation, or is the diploma accredited by a professional body or learned institute other than itself?

Career planning factors

Advantageous

Dramatherapy has proved its worth in many situations where other approaches have failed, so the practitioner is likely to be breaking new ground and has the excitement of using his intelligence and skill to make bridges for his patients to allow them to change their whole patterns of thought and feeling and thus their long established behaviour patterns. Often chance social or professional contacts rather than standard career tracks will lead to an opportunity to introduce art therapy to new groups of sufferers.

The long training and the possibilities for part-time work make the subject one that can suit the timetable of a married woman who may have had to change her career plans to cater for the needs of family life.

Disadvantageous
The same factors that are viewed by one person as advantages can be stumbling blocks for a different personality.

Finance

Discretionary grants are available from some local authorities for professional courses, particularly where the candidate has the backing of a relevant respected local body or national organisation, but you will be dependent on the amount of money available at any one time and on the opinions of the grants committee. Candidates who already have a degree or professional training may be felt to have used up their entitlement to public support. Applications showing the desired training as a logical and necessary career step are most likely to be favourably received. Obtain a place on a course before making application.

Useful addresses

Hertfordshire College of Art and Design, 7 Hatfield Road, St. Albans, Hertfordshire.

See also
Art Therapy, Dance Therapy

Healing

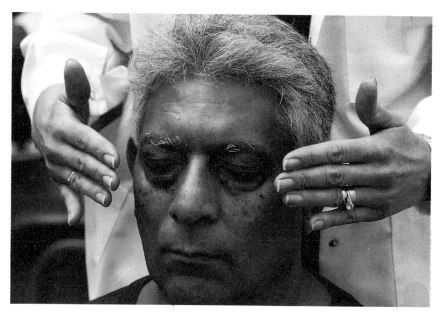

Patients can often feel the same sensations of warmth as are experienced by the healer.

The gift of healing has been reported throughout history, among many different peoples and in many different cultural settings. There is a tendency for religious groups to claim that they alone have been granted the gift by the deity and that healing performed by any other person is diabolically inspired. Much heat is generated by such claims and by attempts to distinguish and allot merit to different types of healing.

It may be helpful to describe, without attempting to evaluate, some of the more familiar features and to comment on some familiar expressions that have a particular significance in this connection.

People who are not familiar with the idea of healing tend to refer to it as faith healing. This expression is not generally used by healers or those accustomed to the phenomenon. Those who use it seem to feel that any change is dependent on the faith of the patient, not on any behaviour of the practitioner.

There is also a suggestion that faith healing is the positive side of a coin of which hysterical illness is the negative. However, this account does not fit cases where animals are healed, as they can hardly be held to have beliefs or faith in the sense intended.

Most healers prefer to call their work spiritual healing, stressing that the activity involves spiritual vital energy, rather than surgery or other physical actions.

Some healing is felt as a draining of energy from the healer to the patient. This is very common among untrained healers.

More practised healers seem to be able to call on a universal power and act as a channel bringing it to the patients without themselves suffering depletion.

Most healers seem to have particular gestures or rituals that they use to help them concentrate and focus on their task. These may include stroking movements, shaking out undesirable energies, moulding the outlines of the body and of what is referred to as its aura. It would be inappropriate here to describe in detail the energy fields that healers describe surrounding the body but most of the gesture patterns refer to this view of the human body and soul as an energetic entity. To what extent this is a metaphor is a matter of contention.

Some healers lay their hands on the patient (hand healing), others give a token such as a flower or coin, others work at a distance by agreement with a patient or a well wisher (absent healing).

Experiments conducted in America by Sister Justa Smith detected changed electrical characteristics of Holy Water compared with tap water and these are often quoted as confirming the description of healing as a transfer of energy.

Although some healing takes place with dramatic suddenness, the sort of change that is referred to as a miracle cure, most healers neither ask for nor expect this. They might look for results ranging from the relief of distress, so as to allow a peaceful death, to an unexpectedly swift recovery from disease or trauma. Experienced healers point out that just as the deterioration in health took place through the natural functions of the body, so the recovery has to use the same means. These would be examples of spiritual healing empowering the natural healing energies of the patient.

The above remarks, simple though they may be, are sure to offend some among the many personalities with experience in this field. Personal experience carries conviction and individuals experience healing differently. Unfortunately the tendency to generalise from individual experience leads people to raise their own perceptions to the status of revelation. Arguments on points of dogma then develop all the animus of religious or scientific debate.

Personality

As has been suggested above, healers vary widely. Is it possible to pick out a characteristic that they have in common? If I can make a personal comment as an outsider, I should say that the characteristic I would pick out is comfortableness. I have met healers who were gardeners, army officers, priests, grooms, dockers, doctors, artists, men and women. Some of them were highly intelligent, others very simple in intellectual terms. All of them had this characteristic of comfortableness. This may have come from a sense that they were open to others, lacking the defensiveness that keeps others at a distance.

Education

No one particular educational background is necessary for a healer, though studies that enable him to express himself clearly and possibly in different sensory modes are likely to be helpful.

Access

A few healers, like Matthew Manning, discover their talent early in life, but most do not take the step of developing it until maturity, even perhaps after retirement.

Career development

As healing is a gift, it seems strange to talk of training for it but if the gift is to be well used there are disciplines and skills that should be learned. It is essential to maintain humility, balance and realism. A valuable gift can be wasted if its bearer succumbs to self-indulgence and hysteria. This personal development is a continuing part of the healer's life. Current thinking suggests that professional training in counselling and communication skills would also be very helpful. A division for Healing Counsellors is open on the British Register of Complementary Practitioners.

Working conditions

Many healers will be satisfied with merely exercising their gift sporadically and freely for the benefit of friends. Others will receive patients but expect only donations to a favourite charity. It is really only appropriate to talk of working conditions for those who are offering a professional service, that is receiving payment for their time and expenses and being prepared to be available on a regular basis at a clinic or in hospitals.

Since 1977 the British Medical Association has allowed healers to visit patients in hospital and in some districts teams of healers are on call where needed. These people work on the same terms as the chaplains who offer spiritual comfort to the sick.

Not every healer can arrange the ideal situation for his work. The late Harry Edwards at his Sanctuary and the late Bruce McManaway at Strathmiglo are two examples of healers who both in their different ways designed the setting that best expressed the nature of their gift and fostered its exercise. Both these healers paid great attention to the development of the gifts of like-minded pupils.

CHECK LIST

- Suppose that you have a healing gift. There will come a point when you will wish to decide what to do about it. Will you simply allow yourself to use it from time to time as an act of charity? Or will you take the step of developing it and offering a professional service to all-comers?
- What are your feelings about the financial side of professional life? If you are to spend time providing a service, you must either have means to live or be able to charge for time you spend with your clients or patients.
- Can you identify the type of person with whom you wish to work? Healing is such an intensely personal skill that for any healer there exists an ideal public.
- What is the type of service that you wish to give? For example, will you work one to one, in small groups or in large meetings? Will you specialise in absent healing or work face to face with your patients?

Career planning factors

Advantageous
This is a career that depends entirely on your own progress

in personal, spiritual development.

There is no set career path. Many healers, however, feel that they are guided in paths that they could never have foretold.

Many who have a highly developed gift for spiritual healing prefer to work professionally in a different field where they can use their gifts as an enhancement of their other skills. This has been the case with many gifted nurses, for example.

Disadvantageous
All the above which seem advantages to many working in spiritual healing are factors that would seem positively disadvantageous to people without this calling.

Finance

You are unlikely to receive grants for training in healing as such but may well be able to find some support for a course designed to enhance your skills in counselling and communication.

Useful address

National Federation of Spiritual Healers, Old Manor Farm Studio, Church Street, Sunbury on Thames, Middlesex TW16 6RG   09327–83164

Books

McManaway, B. & Turcan, J., Healing, 1983, *The Energy that can Restore Health*, Thorsons, London.

Taylor, Allegra 1992, *Healing Hands*, Macdonald Optima, London.

See also
Radionics

Herbal Medicine

Herbal preparations are available as tinctures, teas and in many other forms to be used according to the most convenient method of getting the right level of medication to the patient.

In The Tao of Medicine, *Stephen Fulder makes the interesting point that the drugs discovered in modern pharmacology are bound to be strongly toxic as well as curative because its testing models are* 'sick and unintelligent rats. Safe and subtle remedies can only be fully restored to our culture when self-testing and sensitive observation by practitioners is approved as a method of drug discovery.'

An ironical comment on this is that plant scientists are working against time to catalogue and save the range of useful plants that exist in the world. Professor Ghillian Prance's work at Kew is an important example of this concern. Western pharmacists are, and have traditionally been, interested in naturally occurring therapeutic substances but tend to believe that it is necessary to extract single active ingredients and if possible synthesise them artificially in order to obtain a standard product and work out exact dosages. The medical herbalist on the other hand argues that his plant materials offer a naturally balanced combination of chemicals which offset each other's action and reduce the incidence of damaging side effects. He also argues that the dosage problem is less critical than it appears because his remedies are taken in relatively large quantity and weak dilution. A range of other therapeutic advantages are suggested by the individual cases of different herbs.

Every society has had its own folk pharmacopoeia since time immemorial, but in Britain the professional study of the subject in modern times has been strongly influenced by the settlers in North America who found a range of herbs of great efficacy known to the American Indians. Herbal medicine as taught and practised in Britain now incorporates many of these discoveries, to the neglect of indigenous plants.

Meanwhile in West Africa and South Africa efforts have begun to safeguard the useful plants traditionally in use. Pakistan is the scene of a long-running programme of testing and evaluating traditional plant-based medicines under the auspices of the Hamdard Institute of Karachi and The World Health Organisation has reported on the potential value of these resources for the population of the world. Eastern Europe and the Asian countries have been ready to devote time and funds to research, while comparatively little of a serious kind has been done in Western Europe. China, of course, has preserved a flourishing tradition and after a hiccup when herbal medicine was felt to be connected with the time of the landlords provides proper training for its traditional practitioners and encourages research into their methods.

Personality

The practice of herbal medicine demands many of the qualities that one would look for in a physician. As well as observation, empathy, conscientiousness and skill, precision is important in anyone handling potentially pharmacologically powerful material.

Education

A sound general education with a bias towards biological sciences. Two of these at A level preferred.

Access

Many candidates come as mature students who have accumulated knowledge and skills during previous professional experience. The School is skilled at assessing these and advising where they need to be topped up to allow the candidate to cope with the course.

Medically qualified people can apply for exemption from those parts of the course which their own qualifications already cover.

Career development

Training as a professional medical herbalist takes four years. The course includes basic human sciences, the study of human disease and diagnostic skills as well as subjects specifically relating to the recognition and use of herbs in medicine.

Doctors can take a one year course at the School of Herbal Medicine, concentrating on those aspects of the syllabus that they have not covered in their previous training.

Graduates become eligible to join the National Institute of Medical Herbalists.

Thereafter their choice is how and where to practise, alone or in a group practice. There are a number of long-established and extremely popular herbal medical practices in the country which have taken on several generations of newly qualified herbalists as assistants and later as associates.

The newly qualified practitioner who can gain entry to one of these practices has a flying start in that the basic administration is taken care of by a well-established management scheme and they can concentrate on developing and refining their skills under the guidance of senior practitioners.

The subject of herbal medicine ties in to other aspects of our cultural life in a number of interesting ways and this provides opportunities for the herbal practitioner to develop side interests that can widen his career. The whole subject of health is of interest to everyone and anybody who has a pleasant manner of writing or broadcasting has a readymade audience for a subject such as herbal medicine. The link between health and the idea of plants gives it double appeal as one is immediately connected to other national enthusiasms, history, gardening, botany.

Working conditions

The medical herbalist is perhaps more than most complementary practitioners suspected of being a witch who brews up potions in her kitchen. In fact most practitioners work in professionally run practice rooms and dispense either commercially prepared herbal medicines or dried or preserved herbal materials to their patients with careful instructions for their preparation or use.

CHECK LIST

- It will be seen from what is written above that in many ways the practitioner of herbal medicine is closer to the norms of medical practice than other complementary practitioners. Anyone who has been attracted to the field of complementary medicine in the first place by a temperamental leaning to non-conformity should check whether this is the subject for them before they embark on the demanding course. There is much in the subject that is of great scientific and philosophical interest and the questions that pose themselves are in fact ones that can be tackled and answered given the time, the money and the will. This will either attract you to the subject or distance you emotionally from it.

Career planning factors

Advantageous

As far as can be judged there is more demand for medical herbalists than can be supplied at the moment. The public appreciates the gentleness and effectiveness of the medicines in restoring normal function combined with the thorough approach of the practitioners who are trained to search out root causes of presented problems.

Disadvantageous

Herbs are comparatively cheap even when brought from distant countries. Moreover as they are natural they cannot become the exclusive property of any commercial interest. Most people probably think this is a good thing. However it can only be seen as a threat to those who earn their livelihoods from the development of more and more expensive synthetic drugs. Anyone who works in herbal medicine must therefore be prepared to argue patiently, persuasively and intelligently with those who genuinely misunderstand their work and against those who have every incentive to spread scare stories.

Being the target of propaganda campaigns is wearing in the long term, so considerable mental and emotional stamina are needed.

The stringent requirements laid on the pharmaceutical chemical industry to prove the safety and efficacy of their products unfortunately bear hard on the herbal medical profession. On grounds of cost alone the tests are prohibitive. The Natural Medicines Society is doing excellent work to protect the freedom to prescribe and use herbal medicines and deserves the support of all Herbalists and their patients.

Finance

Discretionary grants are available from some Local Education Authorities.

Useful addresses

National Institute of Medical Herbalists, 41 Hatherley Road, Winchester, Hants SO22 6RR   0962–68776

National School of Herbal Medicine, Bucksteep Manor, Bodle Street Green, Hailsham, East Sussex BN27 4RJ   0323–833812

Books

Fulder, S. 1982, *The Tao of Medicine: Ginseng, Oriental Remedies and the Pharmacology of Harmony*, Inner Traditions International, New York.

Fulder, S. 1988, *Garlic – How to use garlic to protect your heart and circulation*. Thorsons, London.

Grieve and Lyall 1984, *A Modern Herbal*, Penguin, Harmondsworth.

Grigg, Barbara 1983 *Green Pharmacy*, Jill Norman and Hothouse, London.
A distinguished historical survey.

Hallowell, M. 1985, *Herbal Healing, A practical introduction to medicinal herbs*, Ashgrove Press, Bath.

Hoffman, D. 1987, *The Herb User's Guide*, Thorsons, London.

Hoffman, D. 1983, *The Holistic Herbal*, Findhorn Press, Forres.

Kadans, J.M. 1979, *Encyclopedia of Medicinal Herbs*, Thorsons, London.

Lust, J. 1983, *The Herb Book*, Bantam, New York.

Mabey, Richard, et al 1988, *The Complete New Herbal*, Gaia, London.

McIntyre, Anne 1987, *Herbal Medicine*, Macdonald Optima, London.

Mills, S.Y. 1985, *The Dictionary of Modern Herbalism*, Thorsons, London.

**See also
Aromatherapy, Chinese Medicine**

Homoeopathy

Homoeopathy is a form of medical treatment discovered (in 1802) by Samuel Hahnemann, a German doctor who was dismayed at the damage caused by the medicine of his time to his patients. It depends on the theory that like cures like – that is that a minute dilution of a substance that will normally cause a particular illness will actually cure it. This is cross referenced with a system of description of different constitutional types distinguished by Hahnemann. Thus the same illness in different people will not necessarily be treated by the same medicine, but by one appropriate to the person. Medicines are prepared by dilution and by succussion. The physical and pharmacological principles underlying this form of medicine seem to be receiving exciting support from modern physics which is much concerned with the borderlines between form, matter and energy.

Personality

Homoeopathic practitioners are concerned to analyse minutely their patients' behaviour and experiences with a view to choosing the precise remedy necessary. A personality willing to be concerned conscientiously with nuances is essential, as the distinctions made are often subtle but vitally important.

Education

To cope with a full training in classical homoeopathy it is desirable to have the equivalent of two A levels in scientific subjects, one of them being biology. However the colleges and their tutors have experience in assessing the work needed to fill in educational gaps and are able to advise those who might have difficulty.

Access

Training courses for doctors are run in London and Glasgow. These require them to have completed their medical training and then add a short course. Some such courses are very perfunctory and there is now a welcome tendency for some doctors to enrol in courses designed for specialist homoeopaths and omit the parts of the course

covering material already dealt with within their medical
training.

Specialist homoeopaths who have no previous medical
training will undertake a full time course that combines with
their strictly homoeopathic studies material on human
sciences and diagnosis. This usually lasts three and a half or
four years. Arrangements can usually be made after
consultation with the staff to spread the material over a
longer time for people who have particular problems and
need to combine work and study.

Career development

Students will wish to set up practice on their own account as
soon as possible but should consider the wisdom of assisting
first in a practice or clinic where there is a senior practitioner
to advise and possibly help give a start by referring their
patient overload.

A division of the British Register is open for applications
from classical homoeopaths working in the pure
Hahnemannian tradition, irrespective of their place of
training. Applicants should write to the Institute for
Complementary Medicine for the necessary forms as early
as possible so as to see what is required. Theoretically they
are able to apply as soon as they have available notes on ten
cases for which they have taken full responsibility. It is also
important to maintain contact with your training college
partly in order to keep in touch with developments in the
field and also because students who have earned a
reputation for excellence during their training and in their
professional practice are often invited to contribute as
lecturers to following generations of students. Moves are
afoot to weld links between specialist homoeopaths in
different countries. There has always been interchange
between Britain and India (where homoeopathy is a
respected specialism in medical education) but it is now
growing within Europe, including the newly thawed Eastern
bloc countries. From a career point of view this suggests that
there are likely to be opportunities to make international
exchanges, either between colleges and professional
organisations or between individual practitioners.

A homoeopathic physician is traditionally appointed to the royal household.

Working conditions

Increasingly homoeopaths work in professional practice rooms. It used to be that homoeopaths felt that their discipline was so different from anything that any other type of therapy had to offer that they could not work in the same building with any other type of practitioner. This was, of course, particularly true of homoeopathic doctors. Perhaps it is increased confidence in the validity of the subject and in the standards of proficiency achieved that has allowed a change to come about. A growing number of classical homoeopaths are able to share clinic space without finding that either patients or their colleagues are confused about what is going on and a few homoeopathic doctors now feel able to work alongside specialists with no orthodox medical background.

CHECK LIST

- If you are a doctor, discuss with your colleagues the pros and cons of undertaking homoeopathic training and their attitude to your possibly introducing homoeopathy into the practice. In the past they might have been doubtful or unsympathetic. Now they may be glad to have someone in the practice with the competence to offer this type of treatment to patients.
- If you are not a doctor you must be aware that yours will be one of the longest trainings in the range of natural therapies. Check your mental and financial stamina and make sure that you will be able to last the course.
- Check that any homoeopathic course offered you is in fact a classical one. There has grown up a confusion in some minds between homoeopathy and medical herbalism as well as between classical homoeopathy and the use of homoeopathic remedies by practitioners using a variety of alien diagnostic methods.

Career planning factors

Advantageous

For doctors, the opportunity to offer your patients a gentle form of treatment that many of them actually want. An opportunity to spend considerably longer with your patients than is customary in a normal consultation.

Disadvantageous

For doctors, the National Health Service will only fund homoeopathic treatment to patients within your immediate catchment area. Those referred from elsewhere have to be treated privately. Homoeopathic consultations take considerably longer than orthodox consultations.

Finance

Some Local Education Authorities will award partial discretionary grants to those who have not already had a grant for a degree or similar course.

Useful addresses

British Homoeopathic Association, 27a Devonshire Street, London W1N 1RJ   071–935–2163
Linked with Faculty of Homoeopaths.

Faculty of Homoeopathy, Royal London Homoeopathic Hospital, Great Ormond Street, London WC1N 3HR 071–837–3091 × 72
Linked with the British Homoeopathic Association. Accepts only doctors.

London College of Classical Homoeopathy, Morley College, 61 Westminster Bridge Road, London SE1 071–928–6199

Homoeopathic Hospital, 1000 Great Western Road, Glasgow G12 0NR   041–339–0382
Trains doctors and runs programmes with other Glasgow hospitals as well as clinics in the city.

Society of Homoeopaths, 2 Artizan Road, Northampton NN1 4HU   0604–21400

School of Homoeopathic Medicine, (Darlington),
14 Greenfield Place, Ryton, Tyne and Wear NE40 3LT
091–413–2770
New Course coming on stream.

Scottish College of Homoeopathy, 17 Queens Crescent,
Glasgow G4 9BL   041–332–3917

Application forms for the Homoeopathic Division of the
British Register of Complementary Practitioners may be
obtained by writing to the Registrar, c/o The Institute for
Complementary Medicine, (see page 4).

Books

Clover, Dr Anne 1984 *Homoeopathy: A Patient's Guide*,
Thorsons, London

Vithoulkas, George 1985 *Homoeopathy: Medicine for the New Man*, Thorsons, London

Hypnotherapy

Hypnotherapy is often referred to as the art of suggestion. Graham, see below, page 122, lists many misconceptions on the subject and points to similarities and overlaps with other types of mental therapy. Nowadays its usefulness is recognised in helping patients to overcome problems of many different kinds. For example students of all ages can be helped to concentrate and fulfil their potential without distraction and waste of mental effort. In health care the applications are numerous. The following are only a few examples. Helping patients to lose habits such as smoking is probably the most familiar but hypnotherapy can help cure many conditions that are stress related, including infertility. There are records of operations being successfully carried out under hypnosis. Most people would probably prefer to rely on normal anaesthesia for surgery, but there is no doubt of the usefulness of hypnosis in procedures that are uncomfortable but where anaesthesia is impossible for technical reasons. Mastectomy patients and others who feel for some reason that they are repulsive can be saved much emotional distress by hypnotherapeutic help to change their self image. Hospice nurses value hypnotherapy as a means of soothing anxiety and pain, reducing the need for medication. Contrary to popular misconceptions, intelligent people with lively minds stand the best chances of benefiting from hypnotherapy.

Personality

It seems probable that almost anyone is capable of hypnotising others. However more than the simple talent is needed to become a professional hypnotherapist. As with many of the natural therapies, what hypnotherapy seems to do for the patients is to give informaion to the whole person at a very deep level. Considerable intelligence as well as empathy is needed to identify the patient's true need and supply the treatments to complement it. The basic actions needed are often apparently very simple. Empathy and humility are essential personal characteristics for practitioners who carry out these simple actions conscientiously.

Education

Hypnotherapists enter training from a number of educational backgrounds. Many have psychology degrees. A surprising number come from a background of computer studies and there is perhaps an analogy between the planning of suggestions for a patient and the programming of a computer for a particular task. Social workers and teachers are also strongly represented among recruits to the profession.

Access

Several groups including medical doctors and clinical psychologists claim that they are the only people who should be allowed access to the profession of hypnotherapy. However there are no legal restrictions on who may undertake training and practice.

Career development

Training in hypnotherapy will include in a carefully articulated course an understanding of current knowledge of the development of human personality, counselling skills, understanding of the mode of actions of suggestion, the modalities of sensory input, knowledge of a range of hypnotherapeutic techniques and practical training in how to apply them appropriately in different settings.

For nurses, a pioneering course has been started with joint accreditation from the Royal College of Nursing and the Institute for Complementary Medicine, combining some suitable hypnotherapeutic and massage techniques in a module suitable for use on the wards or in a visiting situation. The University of Manchester has accepted this course as part of a Degree in Nursing Studies. Further courses involving hypnotherapy are likely to be developed soon.

There is a Hypnotherapy Division of the British Register of Complementary Practitioners open to any applicant who can satisfy the scrutiny panel of his competence and professional standards. Application forms may be obtained from the Institute for Complementary Medicine.

Hypnotherapists registered with this division undertake six days of in-service training each year and maintain a peer supervision relationship throughout their working lives.

Working conditions

Most hypnotherapists receive their clients in private practice rooms, but there is increasing scope for work in hospitals, especially in clinics dealing with particular problems such as infertility, convalescence from cardiac disease, intractable pain, post-surgical rehabilitation, and so on. Often the practitioner will be required to work as part of a team with doctors or nurses who are carrying out some distressing procedure, rather like a normal anaesthetist. Some of the most rewarding work will be in teaching patients to use the method for themselves so as to enhance their quality of life.

General practitioners are increasingly referring patients to the hypnotherapy practitioners on the British Register of Complementary Practitioners for help with problems such as addiction, anxiety, phobias and general support in coping with their lives. Here again the emphasis is on liberating the patients from habits of mind that are no longer helpful and teaching them how to use hypnotherapeutic methods to help themselves.

CHECK LIST

- Check that any course of training you are offered has a record of getting people on to the British Register of Complementary Practitioners.
- Check that you wish to undertake a course that can be searching in terms of personal revelation and growth and demanding in its academic content. If in doubt find an introductory course in counselling skills and use it to test the water. You may find that a career involving professional intimacy is not for you. If so, it is better to do so early.

Career planning factors

Advantageous
This is a field where maturity is a positive advantage. Many

of the most successful hypnotherapists have entered the field as a second career.

Relations with General Practitioners are generally excellent. Registered hypnotherapists increasingly receive referrals from local doctors.

Sound training is readily available in most parts of the country.

Demand for the treatment is growing.

Disadvantageous
The subject has sometimes been brought into disrepute by music hall stage hypnotists putting on demonstrations in questionable taste.

Similarly attempts have recently been made to set up franchise and multi-level marketing organisations under the titles of either hypnotherapy or stress reduction.

Finance

Some excellent courses are organised round weekend workshops, so it should not be impossible to combine training and earning. A more difficult problem is making the transition from part-time to full-time practice and the ease with which this is accomplished largely depends on the location in which one decides to practise.

Useful addresses

National College of Hypnotherapy and Psychotherapy, 12 Cross Street, Nelson, Lancs   0282–699378

National School of Hypnosis and Advanced Psychotherapy, 28 Finsbury Park Road, London N4 2JX   081–226–6963

Application forms for the Hypnotherapy Division of British Register of Complementary Practitioners may be obtained from the Registrar, c/o The Institute for Complementary Medicine.

Books

Graham, H. *Time, Energy and the Psychology of Healing*, Jessica Kingsley Publishers, London.

Waxman, D. *Hypnosis: a guide for patients and practitioners*, Allen and Unwin.

See also
Stress Reduction, Relaxation, *Autogenic Training*

Kinesiology

Kinesiology is the use of muscle responses to test, diagnose and treat health problems. This body of knowledge has traditionally formed part of the training of a chiropractor. When used by chiropractors or doctors it is generally referred to as Applied Kinesiology.

It is now developing into a speciality on its own and those who use it in this way generally refer to it as simply Kinesiology.

Personality

As this skill has traditionally been linked to medicine or chiropractic it is difficult as yet to make an assessment of those traits that are specific to Applied Kinesiology.

Education

As well as the hands-on skills of the doctor and the chiropractor, an educational background in physics and an interest in the electro-magnetic properties of the human body are a good basis for Applied Kinesiology. Those who already have a training in massage or some other form of bodywork might find it a natural career development.

Access

A chiropractic or medical qualification should be taken first for Applied Kinesiology. Practitioners of other disciplines who want to train now have their own professional body and access to workshops and a training structure.

Career development

Until recently the subject was seen as a specialist interest of practitioners already established in their own fields. This limits the possibilities of career development. However the growth of an internationally linked organisation for training and accreditation of kinesiology practitioners suggest that the picture will change over the next few years. Anyone interested in developing a career in the field should take a beginners' Touch for Health course and join the Kinesiology Federation to keep in touch with developments

in standards, training and the various options that are
opening up.

Working conditions

For chiropractors and doctors in private practice their usual
working conditions will apply. No opportunities yet to use
the technique within the hospital setting.

CHECK LIST

- Check whether you really have the scientific background
  to use this skill with full knowledge. It is easy to be led
  astray in trying to do something that looks very simple.
- Check that any course offering you training in Applied
  Kinesiology is actually accredited with the International
  College in Park City.

Finance

This is not a primary subject on the career path, therefore
grants will not be available.

Useful addresses

International College of Applied Kinesiology, PO Box
680547, Park City, Utah, 84068, USA
for doctors or chiropractors

International Kinesiology College, Lehenstrasse 36,
Zurich, Switzerland, CH 8037
British Contact: Adrian Voce, 8 Railey Mews, Kentish
Town, London NW5 2PA   071–482–0698

Kinesiology Federation, 30 Sudeley Road, Bognor Regis,
West Sussex PO21 1ER

International Association of Specialised Kinesiologists,
859 N. Hollywood Way, Suite 156, Burbank, CA 91505,
USA

International College of Applied Kinesiology, 54 East
Street, Andover, Hants SP10 1ES

Books

Diamond, John, MD 1979, *Behavioural Kinesiology*, Harper & Row

Valentine, Tom and Carol 1985, *Applied Kinesiology*, Thorsons, London.

See also
Touch for Health

Massage

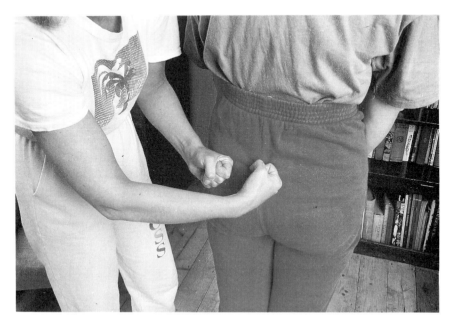

Some forms of massage are less passive than others. This biodynamic treatment involves the patient and the practitioners interacting.

Massage practitioners have long resented the slurs on their profession whereby massage parlour has a sleazy connotation. Massage is an ancient and very effective type of treatment which exists in all cultures in one form or another. Modern Western massage is derived from HP Ling's Swedish (Classical) Massage, which achieved official recognition in 1814.

Personality

Because massage is so widespread there are many different nuances and people of many different kinds can find a niche to suit them. For instance, some will prefer a more intuitive approach and be most interested in the therapy's potential for soothing and relaxing, others will combine their care for the patient with a deep interest in the biochemistry of muscle metabolism.

Massage practitioners are generally practical people who literally want to get their hands on. Their speciality involves doing something apparently simple very well and they develop a strong intuition in interpreting the body language of their patients and colleagues.

Education

Obviously it is helpful for the trainee to have some knowledge of human anatomy and physiology before embarking on a training course, but it is possible to learn what is needed during training.

Access

It is possible to train at any age. Courses with a variety of emphases are available all over the country. It is important to compare a wide selection of brochures to make sure that the course emphasises the areas in which you are most interested and that the level of competence is right. There are many courses leading to qualifications at beauty salon level and others designed for practitioners who may be looking after people who are seriously ill.

Career development

Massage can be seen as the all-purpose, portable skill. It is an excellent first skill to which many others can be added. Those who wish to continue long-term training can earn with their massage while they study.

Some people know immediately which line of interest they want to pursue, but it is not necessary to make up your mind from the start. Possible options include helping sportsmen and women and athletes increase the efficiency of their muscular output of energy and reduce damage to their soft tissues caused by the enormous strain to which they are constantly subjected; helping patients recover after operations, soothing pain and bringing relaxation to patients with terminal illnesses; helping people who have become obese through illness or perhaps psychological trauma shed fat as an adjunct to their dietary regime; bringing people who have been subjected to prolonged strain or a sedentary life back to fitness. Swedish massage was originally developed as a passive version of exercise. This may help explain why massage has a part to play in cleansing the bodily tissues, improving circulation and renewing vitality.

As well as teaching their skills to the next generation, massage practitioners often become the link practitioner between others. They tend to be practical people with a talent for human relations, so moving on to be owners or managers of clinics is a natural career development for them.

There is ample evidence of the usefulness of massage for people with many different types of disability and this is probably a growth area for the future. Traditionally massage has been a speciality for blind practitioners, particularly in the East.

Massage is one of the therapies included in the first course jointly accredited by the Institute for Complementary Medicine and the Royal College of Nursing. It is presented as part of a module for a degree from Manchester University.

A division of the British Register of Complementary Practitioners is open for Massage practitioners. Application forms can be obtained from the Institute for Complementary Medicine.

Working conditions

These will vary widely from private clinics to sports clubs to hospitals. Some practitioners will travel with athletes for months at a time, caring for individuals or teams with the same sort of involvement as a racehorse trainer. Others will build up their clientele in their own home district and derive great satisfaction from following clients through their lives from the tennis-induced sprain, through pregnancy, help with slimming to relief of arthritic stiffness.

It is tempting to many women to choose to work at home or visiting clients. Think carefully about this from a safety point of view as embarrassing and even dangerous situations can arise. As well as the personal distress, any misunderstandings about the nature of the services on offer are highly damaging from a business point of view. If possible it is best to preserve your professional standing by working in a clinic where other practitioners are within call and the setting is so obviously respectable that no trouble of this kind is possible.

CHECK LIST

- Check the level of any training course you may be offered. Is it appropriate to work in a beauty salon or will it give you the necessary competence for helping people who may be seriously ill.
- Do you actually *like* physical contact with people? It may seem a foolish question, but if you have never actually considered it, take a short course to test yourself. You will not lose anything by doing this and may learn a lot about yourself.
- Check your own general physical health and stamina. Many types of massage are physically demanding. You will be taught the correct methods but the work is still often heavy and the hours can be long.

Career planning factors

Advantageous
The variety and flexibility of the subject mean that there are opportunities almost anywhere in the world.

Little equipment is needed.

This is a very human form of care that one can offer one's fellow beings.

Disadvantageous
There are few obvious ladders for promotion. Practitioners have to be alert to opportunities and often make their own openings.

The massage parlour image persists.

Poor technique can cause repetitive strain injury.

Finance

Grants are not likely to be available, but investigate the possibilities available locally in a flexible spirit. For instance, be prepared to think of yourself as a small business starting up or as a student, according to which is most likely to attract support. Many courses are arranged so that people need not give up employment while training.

Useful addresses

Clare Maxwell Hudson School of Massage, 87 Dartmouth Road, London NW2   081–450–6494

College of Holistic Medicine, 4 Craigpark, Glasgow, G31 2NA   041–554–5808
Contact: Mr J.R. Downie, Administrator

Dancing Dragon School, 115 Manor Road, London N16 5PB   081–800–0471
Contact: Su Fox

London School of Sports Massage Ltd., 88 Cambridge Street, London SW1V 4QG   071–234–5962 or 071–834–1849

Northern Institute of Massage, 100 Waterloo Road, Blackpool, Lancs FY4 1AW   0253–403548

Books

Hudson, Clare Maxwell 1988, *The Complete Massage Book*, Dorling Kindersley, London.

Ylinen, Dr Jari and Cash, Mel 1988, *Sports Massage*, Stanley Paul, London.

McTimoney Chiropractic

This type of therapy derives from a split in the chiropractic movement. The chiropractors of the type represented by the British Chiropractic Association (sometimes referred to by McTimoney practitioners as American chiropractic) have always resented the use of the term chiropractic by the users of the McTimoney method and the McTimoney practitioners have insisted on this, considering themselves to represent a more faithful version of the original therapy. The method is a gentle one particularly recommended for back care for people who are in delicate health.

Unfortunately a further split has developed among McTimoney practitioners.

Personality

A self-reliant character and a willingness to think laterally in dealing with health problems is ideally needed for work in this field. Many of these practitioners also evince deeply intuitive and spiritual qualities.

Education

Two science A levels are preferred.

Access

Practitioners who undertake this training come from many different walks of life. Even more markedly than with other forms of natural therapy they do so as a result of experiencing the benefits of the treatment for themselves. A large proportion of entrants are starting a second career and their previous experience and mature understanding of human problems are seen as advantages.

Career development

Tuition at the McTimoney Chiropractic School is scheduled so as to allow students to continue in their employment while learning. Formal classes take place one day a month. This is supported by clinic days when learning continues in an established practice and by a programme of home study.

Senior practitioners play an important part in the training of the next generation.

Working conditions

A glance at the practitioners' directory shows that many of those listed live in the country. A proportion serve a wide rural area by holding clinics in different locations on different days of the week.

Career planning factors

Advantageous
Training can be undertaken by those in employment.
The treatment is very gentle.

Disadvantageous
Splits in the movement can have adverse effects on the morale and stability of the profession.

The way the training is organised may expose practitioners to criticism as part-timers. This is unfair as the standard of performance achieved should be the criterion for assessing the worth of any training rather than the scheduling of the training sessions.

Finance

Grants are unlikely to be available for this type of training within the foreseeable future.

Useful address

McTimoney Chiropractic School Ltd., 14B Park End Street, Oxford OX1 1HH   0865–246786
Linked with Institute of Pure Chiropractic.

Books

Courtney, Anthea 1989, *Chiropractic*, Penguin, Harmondsworth

Naturopathy

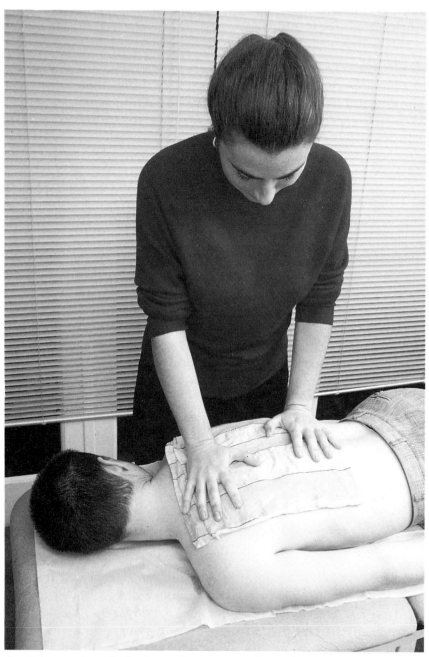

Applying packs to help the patient remove the toxins from his system.

Please note: *In Britain Naturopathy refers to one particular type of practice. In the rest of Europe the same word is used to refer generally to the whole range of skills that are referred to here as complementary medicine. It is therefore important to check what is meant if a European uses this word.*

The naturopath takes as his starting point an idea that underlies many of the natural therapies: that the healthy body resists disease and regulates and repairs itself. His skill involves supporting and stimulating the patient's own vital powers using only the normal means of life: light, air, water, exercise, rest, nourishment and fasting. The treatments will be designed for each patient as an individual after detailed examination and interview to determine the constitution with which he has been endowed by nature as well as to make a diagnosis in the normal sense of the word.

The theory of naturopathy as it has been developed over the past century gives a detailed account of the correspondence between different levels of vitality or its exhaustion and different types of disease. The aspect of this that is most unfamiliar is probably the idea that some illnesses are in fact signs of vitality in that they are manifestations of the body's resistance to attack.

In some ways naturopathy has suffered from its success in that many of its tenets have been taken into popular wisdom about health and hygiene and are no longer thought of as being specifically naturopathic. One needs to look back to the nineteenth century with its stuffy rooms, tight lacing and multiple petticoats for women, stiff clothing for men and heavy meals to see how revolutionary the first naturopaths must have seemed. They let fresh air and sunlight into houses, advocated loose, comfortable clothing made of easily cleaned materials, daily bathing and light meals of fresh wholefoods.

Personality

The naturopath is probably the nearest equivalent in the world of complementary medicine to the general practitioner in orthodox medicine. Naturopaths exercise a range of skills and may work in an outpatient clinic, a residential clinic or nursing home. A well rounded personality is needed, someone who is interested in tackling problems with a high intellectual content in a practical way.

The work is physically, emotionally and intellectually demanding, so good health is necessary. Above all the

student should be a good communicator because he will
spend his life teaching his patients how to be well.

Education

The naturopath needs a sound scientific basis combined
with skill in communication. His emphasis will always be on
educating his patient to be well and this will involve
explanation of what may have gone wrong and instruction
on how to live so as to avoid such troubles in the future.

Access

A levels in Biology, Chemistry and Physics with O level in
English or equivalent are needed to gain entry to the British
College of Naturopathy and Osteopathy.

Career development

After taking a four year course at the British College of
Naturopathy and Osteopathy the student can gain a
Diploma in Naturopathy. For those fortunate enough to
have a family connection the next step will be easy. About 60
percent of new practitioners start as assistant to an
established practitioner for at least part of their time or find
employment position in a residential clinic before they set
up on their own.

There seems to be ample evidence that there is a demand
for the sort of naturopathic centre common elsewhere in
Europe where people can go for a rest and a period of
detoxification. If this demand can be met the future for
naturopaths would be rosy. Such a development has
hitherto been hindered by factors including the peculiar
structure of the British property market and by the
difficulties of regulation and definition that make it hard to
clarify the legal position. If these can be cleared up,
naturopaths will be able to work in a suitable environment,
neither nursing home nor fat farm.

Public interest in matters of health care is endless so
practitioners with a gift for communication may find that
they are able to follow many succesful colleagues into the
fields of writing or broadcasting. Unfortunately the format

of the brains trust where people ring in with problems for a solution does not display the naturopath's holistic approach at its best, but it does give her or him a chance to show that quite simple self-help methods can relieve pain and give the patient a chance to take charge of his own condition.

Working conditions

These vary from the clinic contained within a private home to clinics such as Auchenkyle at Troon, to country house facilities such as Tyringham Clinic. Partnerships of father and son are common; three generations in practice at a time are not unknown.

CHECK LIST

- Naturopathy or equivalent words are used in most European countries to denote any of a number of different types of natural therapy and not in the specific sense that it is used in Britain. Always double check in conversations across language barriers.
- The training is long. Check that you have the resources to hold out financially and make contingency plans in case you need to earn some extra cash. Acting as holiday relief for receptionists or practice secretaries can help pay the bills and also give valuable insights into the day to day problems of practice management.

Career planning factors

Advantageous

The approach is a satisfying and holistic one.

The subject has been studied extensively since the last century so that there is a body of accumulated knowledge.

Patients are interested in the low technology approach, the emphasis on positive action for health and the opportunities for controlling their own destinies.

Disadvantageous

Problems over funding, but these are probably temporary. Slight public suspicion that the ideas are cranky.

Finance

Until recently it has been common to find Local Education Authorities willing to support students with grants. However, following the imposition of the Community Charge, grants have been progressively reduced towards the minimum. With so many areas of Local Government in a state of flux, it is difficult to predict how future students will be treated.

Useful addresses

British Naturopathic and Osteopathic Association, Frazer House, 6 Netherhall Gardens, London NW3 5RR 071–435–6464

British College of Naturopathy and Osteopathy, Frazer House, 6 Netherhall Gardens London NW3 5RR

Books

Lindlahr, H. 1975, *Philosophy of Natural Therapeutics*, Maidstone Osteopathic Clinic, Maidstone.

Turner, Roger Newman 1990, *Naturopathic Medicine*, Thorsons, London.

Seyle, H. 1976, *The Stress of Life*, McGraw-Hill, Toronto.

See also
Nutrition, Osteopathy, *Hydrotherapy*

Opportunities for Nurses

Nurses are taking an increasing interest in the natural therapies for several reasons.

They are the people who get left with the patients for whom doctors can do no more. They know that complementary medicine can help them give desperately ill people an improved quality of life even if it is at the end of life.

They see first hand the side effects of some modern medicine. While no one would undervalue the sometimes almost miraculous work done by surgeons and physicians, one cannot ignore the price that sometimes has to be paid for it.

Most of them came into nursing in order to give personal care to their patients. Now they tend to find that they are required to do many things to and for them that are technical and possibly unpleasant or frankly painful. They welcome the chance to offer their patients care that brings them into personal contact again, relieves distress and builds a relationship that makes painful treatments less distressing if later they become necessary.

Many of them are convinced by personal experience of the efficacy of these methods.

Personality

Nurses have been trained to work scrupulously even in minute and simple matters. Their humility and dedication make them excellent students of the complementary therapies.

Education

The changes in the education of nurses now under way are likely to make them all the more suited to take any of the training courses leading to professional status as a complementary practitioner. At present it is probably the registered nurses who are in the best position to go straight into professional training courses. Enrolled nurses would need to supplement their basic scientific education for most of the subjects.

Access

The Institute for Complementary Medicine and the Royal College of Nursing have just jointly developed and accredited the first of a series of courses to be offered as part of a degree course for Manchester University. This module is an introduction to skills in massage and hypnotherapy that are suitable for nurses to use in their wards or in a visiting situation. Both these skills have much to offer in soothing distress and anxiety and relieving pain. Further courses will follow, all of them aimed specifically at nurses and leading them on to a later stage when they may wish to take the full professional courses that lead to independent practitioner status.

Career development

Many nurses leave the profession either for a child-rearing period or for good after a few years. If they have taken modules of training in complementary therapies as part of their nursing education, they are well on the way to a second career. Once they have completed their full training to become professional practitioners, and are registered with the appropriate section of the British Register of Complementary Practitioners, they are in a strong position to offer their services to their local General Practitioners, not as subordinates but as professionals in their own right. The relationship is all important because the complementary practitioner must be able to make her own assessment of what she can do to help the patient rather than be ordered to give something that may be inappropriate. The growth of independent fund holders and changes in thinking about what should be available on the National Health Service should make for a more flexible attitude to the payment of fees to individual practitioners for services to patients.

Working conditions

In hospitals and homes alike conditions may not be right for the deployment of the full skills of any one of the complementary therapies. However, it is possible to learn appropriate skills that can be deployed without any need for particular equipment or accommodation.

Some hospitals are now taking the first steps towards employing specialist practitioners of the various complementary skills. When this happens the practitioner should take care to specify what accommodation and equipment are necessary in order to do a proper job before the event. Nurse practitioners are used to putting up with conditions in hospitals, but they also have their accumulated knowledge of how the system works to help them get the conditons right first.

CHECK LIST

- If you are looking at a course, check what level of practice it is aimed at. There are some excellent courses designed for the health and beauty industry or salon setting which are not necessarily right for anyone who may be treating people who are seriously ill or who wishes to set up later as a specialist practitioner.
- Check whether there is already a course that gains you a credit towards a degree in nursing studies. The Institute of Advanced Nursing Education will be able to tell you the latest position.
- Check that your superiors and colleagues know that you have done a properly accredited course. There has been so much informal passing on of tips between friends in the past that people are understandably confused about standards and can take a negligent attitude to nurses who practise complementary skills.

Career planning factors

Advantageous
A relief for the practitioner from impersonal styles of care. A second career that can be planned to fit in with family commitments.

A way of enhancing skills and qualifications.

A way of improving relationships with patients.

Fits in with new status of nurses as independent health care professionals.

Disadvantageous
Possibility of nurse being treated as subordinate partner in

care. This is a diminishing risk but one that has been powerful in the past.

Finance

With improved accreditation of course and government's avowed encouraging attitude to self selection of training and career advancement it should be possible to gain at least tax relief on course fees. If in doubt consult an accountant about your personal position.

Useful address

The Registry, **Institute of Advanced Nursing Studies**, c/o Royal College of Nursing, Cavendish Square, London W1   071–409–3333

See also
Hypnotherapy, Massage

Nutrition

Food plays a part in most of the religions of the world and what we put into ourselves literally becomes the fabric of our selves. It is thus no surprise that many illnesses arise from either faulty nutrition or from a failure to absorb what is being eaten. The relationship between health and happiness and nutrition is a two way one. A professional nutritional adviser will need to consider whether the patient feels ill or unhappy because he is feeding poorly or whether illness or unhappiness is upsetting his nutritional intake.

Personality

The nutritionist who wants to work offering his or her knowledge direct to the public, rather than at the laboratory bench, needs to combine a strong scientific interest in the subject with a warm and supportive personality. The Bible says: 'Better a dinner of herbs where love is than a stalled ox and hatred therewith.'

Education

Ideally a first science degree in one of the biological sciences or two scientific A levels.

Access

For any university course in nutrition consult the Registrar of the appropriate department. For a private course you will probably be required to attend an interview if you have neither of the educational qualifications above. Do not be tempted to accept a place on a course just because you have been given it if you think you may have difficulties. It may be better to get a better foundation first. See 'Access Courses' in the glossary section of this book, page 156, for suggestions.

Career development

Private courses available usually take two years and are taught at a series of weekend workshops to allow the students to continue their normal work.

University courses (MA and BSc) tend to be concerned to describe the process of nutrition rather than to aid the student to apply the knowledge to real life cases. During the professorship of John Yudkin, London University offered an excellent practical course. It is to be hoped that similar courses can be stimulated again in response to current interest in the subject.

When setting up as a nutritional consultant, it is important to be clear about what you are doing. There has been a certain amount of adverse press comment on the tendency to see nutritional advice as concerned with the selling of dietary supplements. They are not at all the same thing. Supplements can be very useful precisely as supplements when for some reason the patient cannot obtain the nutrition he needs from the food available but nutritional advisers aim to lead their patients towards the state where they are obtaining everything they need in ample quantities from their normal food intake.

Working conditions

Nutritional advice combines happily with many other different types of natural therapy and the practitioner who is skilled in personal relations will usually be a welcome team member in a mixed clinic. One city clinic, for example, has a medical doctor, a McTimoney practitioner and a nutritional consultant working together. Such a team is well equipped to work either together or individually and support each others' special skills.

CHECK LIST

- If considering a university course ask how much it is geared to practical applications of scientific knowledge.
- If looking at a private course check your impressions of the staff involved. Make sure you speak to them personally as well as inspecting brochures. Check that you are really being trained as an independent professional practitioner and not as a salesmen for supplements. If the training organisation actually recommends its own range of vitamins, minerals, and so on, what is the relationship between the course and the products?

Career planning factors

Advantageous
This is a portable skill.

It involves many aspects of your personality and different types of skills, scientific, analytical, interpersonal and problem solving.

Even if you do not wish to be a consultant the knowledge gained in training can be used in many different settings, in the family or in running a variety of small businesses.

Disadvantageous
A slight suspicion lingers in the public mind over the selling methods of some suppliers of dietary supplements. This is probably not justified but can be embarrassing.

Finance

It should be possible to finance a private course by working while training. University courses should attract local authority grants if you have not had one of these before.

Useful addresses

British Nutrition Foundation, 15 Belgrave Square, London SW1X 8PS   071–235–4904

Centre for Nutritional Studies, The Garden House, Rufford Abbey, Newark, Notts NG22 9DE   0623–822004

Institute for Optimum Nutrition, 5 Jerdon Place, London SW6 1BE   081–385–7984
Courses for nutritional advisers.

McCarrison Society, 23 Stanley Court, Worcester Road, Sutton, Surrey.
Research into relationship between health and nutrition

For optical problems: **Nutritional Eye Health Centre**, Sanctuary House, Oulton Road, Oulton NR32 4QZ Lowestoft 83294

Books

Llewellyn-Jones, D. 1980, *Every Body, a Nutritional Guide to Life*, OUP.

Mayes, A. 1985, *Dictionary of Nutritional Health*, Thorsons, London.

Null, G. 1984, *The Complete Guide to Health and Nutrition*, Arlington, London.

See also
Naturopathy

Osteopathy

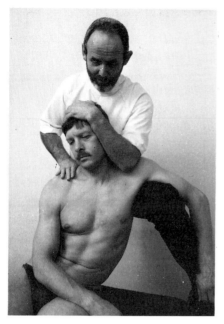

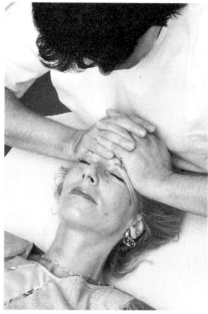

It is the direction more than the force that is important in osteopathic treatment. Here the practitioner is supplying support to the patient so that the thrust is entirely controlled.

Cranial osteopathy.

Osteopathy is one of the manipulative therapies developed in the Mid-West of the United States of America at the end of the nineteenth century when orthodox medical treatment was poor and in short supply. The original theory propounded by Andrew Still in 1874 was that almost all ills suffered by human beings were attributable to osteopathic lesion or subluxations, damage of some kind to a joint which could lead to stiffness, imperfect circulation and a train of adverse consequences and also hinder the body's natural ability to overcome infections.

While few osteopaths nowadays make such far-reaching claims for their art, they are widely valued for their ability to help with back pain, joint and muscle problems and for their sound anatomical understanding. Less widely known and understood is their work on problems such as hyperactivity in children, spasticity, Bell's palsy, trigeminal neuralgia and menstrual problems.

In the United States of America the American Medical Association waged a ferocious campaign against osteopathy for many years until in 1955 their representatives were invited to visit five of the osteopathic colleges and had to admit that the curriculum was almost identical with their own with the addition of some specifically osteopathic material.

In Britain osteopathy is learned by doctors in a short add-on course and by other pupils in a four or five year course which includes anatomy, physiology and pathology as well as the practice of osteopathic manipulation.

Personality

Osteopaths tend to be active by inclination, with independence of mind and a willingness to make their own assessments and act on them.

Education

A broad general education with a scientific bias is required.

Access

To cope successfully with an osteopathic course a minimum of two scientific A levels is required. However, all too many people who would make excellent osteopaths have been deprived of the necessary scientific foundations and the schools are experienced in helping candidates make up deficits of this kind. Moreover, a considerable proportion of students are re-training with a view to starting a second career. They should not be discouraged by lack of formal qualification, but ask for their prior learning and experience to be assessed.

Career development

After qualification most students seek work as assistant to a senior practitioner before setting up in their own practice. Often it will be both more interesting and financially advantageous to have a day in different places, particularly at the beginning of the career. Some practitioners, for example, work predominantly in the suburbs, but do one day a week in a more expensive practice room in central London. Others who live in the country may serve a wide area by practising on different days of the week in different market towns.

Personal interests will obviously play a major part in deciding where to practise but country practitioners may find themselves helping people who have hurt themselves through accidents or repetitive strain at work, whereas towns and suburbs yield a crop of injuries from sudden exertion by the sedentary.

There are a number of specialities in which practitioners may develop a special interest and it is possible to take post graduate courses in subjects such as *cranial osteopathy*. Often friendly co-operation with colleagues in related subjects such as physiotherapy is possible. Some practitioners develop special expertise in helping women recovering from childbirth or coping with the menopause. A number of menstrual problems that have been attributed to biochemical causes yield to gentle manipulation of the pelvis.

An Osteopathic Division of the British Register is open for applications. Write to the Institute for Complementary Medicine for details.

Working conditions

Most osteopaths work in a conventional practice room, but some who have special expertise in the problems of dancers or athletes can be found in dance studios or sports clubs. Some theatres have attached osteopaths who keep performers under supervision checking for signs of strain or possible problems so that damage can be prevented at an early stage.

CHECK LIST

● Have you the independence of mind to keep up your professional standards while working on your own? Although the modern trend is for more communication between practitioners and between people in different types of work, many osteopaths, particularly in rural areas, still work on their own.

- Are you prepared to continue training on other subjects in order to widen the spectrum of services that you can offer your clients? The osteopath is often consulted about subjects wide of his speciality and there is a temptation to offer advice without a full professional basis.
- Check that your career plans fit your circumstances. Do you need to move in order to make contact with the type of patients in whom you are most interested?

Career planning factors

Have you considered what type of career you want? You may wish to remain as a practitioner in daily contact with patients, to specialise in particular subjects or groups of patients or to go on to teach your skills to others or to spend part of your time communicating with the public or print or through the media. Decisions about where you work and live will depend on your wishes in these respects. For example somone who is mainly interested in the problems of sportsmen might want to move away from a south coast resort that would suit someone interested in arthritis and the problems of the elderly.

Finance

Partial grants have been available for osteopathic training. The recognition of the degree status of some courses should improve and extend this support but some confusion may be expected during the changes that will take place over the next few years.

Useful addresses

British College of Naturopathy and Osteopathy, Frazer House, 6 Netherall Gardens, London, NW3 5RR 071–435–7830

British Osteopathic Association, 8–10 Boston Place, London NW1 6QH   071–262–5250
Linked with London College of Osteopathic Medicine. Admits only doctors.

British School of Osteopathy, 1–4 Suffolk Street, London SW1Y 4HG   071–930–9254

London School of Osteopathy, 110 Lower Richmond Road, London SW15   081–788–1991

Society of Osteopaths, 62 Bower Mount Road, Maidstone, Kent   0622–674656
Linked with European School of Osteopathy.

Books

Masters, Paul 1989, *Osteopathy for Everyone*, Penguin, Harmondsworth

Sadler, Stephen 1987, *Osteopathy*, Macdonald Optima, London.

See also
Cranial Osteopathy

Reflexology

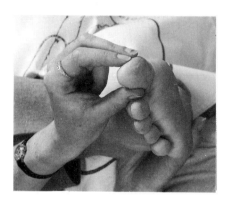

The practitioner has identified the areas of the foot needing special attention to promote healing.

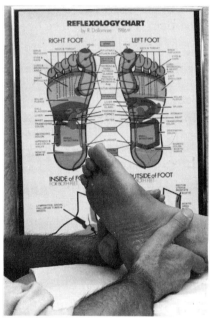

Reflexology as it is known today is based on the work of Eunice Ingham, who in the 1930s charted the pressure points on the feet recognised today. These and the corresponding ones on the hands are the points that most reflexologists use in treating people with a variety of health problems. However, Mrs Ingham was developing work begun in the nineteenth century in America and in Europe and even this seems to have been long pre-dated. Paintings in Egyptian tombs apparently show Nubian practitioners giving many different kinds of medical treatment, including foot reflexology. There are also obvious parallels with much that is taught in Chinese medicine.

Personality

Patience, a pragmatic and conscientious attitude are needed. We do not yet know how reflexology works. A clear mind is needed to draw useful conclusions from what is found on examination of the feet and to plan appropriate treatment.

Education

No formal educational requirements.

Access

Access to courses is usually by interview. The tutors need to be assured that the students are prepared to work seriously at detailed work, both on the practical and on the theoretical side.

Career development

Reflexology is popular with the public though they often have strange ideas of what it is and what it can do. Because of the growth in the number of practitioners working at salon level, it tends to be confused with various minor massage procedures.

Length of training depends on the aptitude of the practitioner and on the organisation of the course provider. A list of training organisations is given below. From reading their brochures you will see that they make different assumptions about what you already know. This will account for differences in length of course. Some allow you to repeat material as often as you wish until it is mastered. Others assume that you will have done so by a specific time.

Independent practitioners are becoming increasingly recognised and there are good opportunities to build up a faithful clientele particularly if you are fortunate enough to happen upon a spectacular case where this type of therapy is highly effective, as in speeding recovery from car crash injuries. Particularly in country areas word of mouth following a successful treatment can do wonders.

A Reflexology Division of the British Register of Complementary Practitioners is open to receive applications. Write for details to the Institute for Complementary Medicine.

Working conditions

Some practitioners specialise in visiting their patients in the home. If this is done it must be costed so as to pay for travel expenses. Others practise in professional practice rooms or attach themselves to a clinic. No particular equipment is required except suitable chairs at a correct height for both patient and practitioner and possibly a means of supporting the patient's leg so that the reflexologist does not suffer from backache. A lavish supply of clean towels is essential.

CHECK LIST

● Visit a practitioner as a patient and check that you find the type of work attractive.
● Check the assumptions that any training organisation is making about your prior competence before entry so as to match the course to your needs.

Career planning factors

Advantageous
Popular subject with the public.
Skill is portable.
No particular educational requirements.

Disadvantageous
More research needs to be done as to underlying rationale of the treatment and on verifying the map of the points.

Confusion caused in the past in the public mind from lack of systematic recording of cases.

Finance

Courses are generally organised on a reversed week or weekend workshop basis so should not interfere with current job committments.

Useful addresses

Bayley School of Reflexology, Monks Orchard, Whitbourne, Hereford and Worcester WR6 5RB
0886–21207
Contact: Secretary Nicola M. Hall

British School for Reflex Zone Therapy of the Feet, 97 Oakington Avenue, Wembley Park, London
HA9 8HY   081–908–2201
Affiliated to a body in Germany (ISRZTF). Trains only doctors and nurses. Can supply addresses of practitioners in many districts of British Isles.
Contact: Secretary, Mrs Ann Lett

British School of Reflexology, PO Box 34, Dept. NH, Harlow, Essex   0279–29060
Contact: Secretary, Mrs E.A. Gillanders-Burgess.

Midland School of Reflex Therapy, 5 Church Street, Warwick CB34, 4AS   0926–491–071
Contact: Principal Christine Jones, MCSP, MRSH

Raworth Centre, 20/26 South Street, Dorking, Surrey   0306–742150
Contact: Principal: Mrs M. Raworth. This centre teaches a course combining reflexology, aromatherapy, first aid and other therapies.

Hoths School for Holistic Therapy, 39 Prestbury Road, Pittville, Cheltenham, Gloucestershire GL52 2PT 0242–512601

Mary Martin School of Reflexology, 37 Standale Grove. Ruislip, Middlesex HA4 7UA   0895–635621

Larger College of Reflexology, 41 Parkfield, New Ross, Co. Wexford, Ireland   051–22209

House of Healing, 87 The Lookout, Chepstow, Gwent NP6 5BL   02912–6064

Crane School of Reflexology, 135 Collins Meadow, Harlow, Essex CM19 4EJ   0279–21682

Lillian Stoltenberg School of Holistic Reflexology, 96 Pennsylvania Rd., Exeter EX4 6DQ   0392–219798

Books

Hall, Nicola 1986, *Reflexology*, Thorsons, London.

Gore, Anya 1982, *Reflexology*, Macdonald Optima, London.

See also
Chinese Medicine

Glossary

Access courses

These are courses designed to help pupils gain access to courses from which they would otherwise be excluded by providing instruction that will fill the gaps left by their previous education. City of Westminster College offers an evening course of six modules specifically designed to help those who have been deprived of basic mathematical or scientific skills reach a standard suitable for acceptance on to courses in Acupuncture, Herbal Medicine, Homoeopathy, Nutrition and Osteopathy. Anyone interested should ring 071–723–9312 and ask for details of the course on Preparing to Train in Alternative Medicine.

Acupressure

Technique of using finger or tool pressure on the same points as **Acupuncture**. It is usually taught in courses on **Acupuncture** and **Chinese Medicine**. q.v.

Auricular therapy

A specialist technique based on Chinese acupuncture and acupressure techniques, but also drawing on Western reflex zone theory. The ear is regarded as a map of the whole body and reflex points used to affect improvement in the desired zones. It has a reputation of success in cases of addiction and may be helpful in supporting those who wish to withdraw from tranquillisers. For details of training contact Roger Rose, Secretary, 37 Great Northern Road, Dunstable, Bedforshire LU5 4BN Tel: 0582–668417.

Autogenic training

Method of teaching relaxation of muscles and control of involuntary physical processes such as circulation, heart and pulse rates, using a combination of psychological and physiological knowledge. Autogenic training has the reputation of being the method of relaxation training preferred by doctors, perhaps because of what may appear to others to be its rather rigid approach. However, those with experience in other methods will recognise its congruence with phenomena recognised by, for example, yogis, hypnotherapists, shamans, healers and the religious of many different cultures and indeed with methods arrived at intuitively by uninstructed human beings. It is used to help those subject to prolonged stress and nervous tension control their physical and emotional reactions and so take the control of their lives that they may feel they have lost. H.J. Schultz's method of autogenic training is widely used to relieve pain and prevent physical and emotional damage to mother and child during childbirth. For a detailed account of this use see Umberto Piscicelli, *Respiratory Autogenic Training and Obstetric Psychoprophylaxis*, Piccin, Padua, 1987, ISBN 88–299–0242–X. Women who would like to use this method of help in their own confinements should contact the National Childbirth Trust, Alexandra House, Oldham Terrace, London W3. Tel: 081–992–8637. For training in the use of autogenic training for general relaxation and stress reduction contact Centre for Autogenic Training, 10 Harley Street, London W1.   Tel: 071–935–1811.

Bach flower remedies
A series of remedies for emotional disorders created by Dr Edward Bach from water potentised with the therapeutic frequency of different plants in sunlight. The procedure has points in common with the potentisation of homoeopathic remedies by succussion. The remedies are often used for the emotional support of patients who are being treated for physical ills by naturopathic or other means. However they may be thought to work, they have the great advantages of being harmless and easy to use. Many families keep a set of the remedies in their first aid kit and it seems that most of the remedies produced are in fact self-prescribed and administered. For these reasons they are unlikely to form the basis of a professional career. For Bach flower remedies and information on their use write to: Bach Flower Remedies, Mount Vernon, Stotwell, Wallingford OX10 0PZ. Tel: 0491–39489. An account of the remedies and the story of their discovery may be found in: Hyne-Jones, T.W. *Dictionary of Bach Flower Remedies*, Banstead, 1977 and Weeks, Norah, *The Medical Discoveries of Edward Bach, Physician*, C.W. Daniel, Saffron Walden, 1973.

Biofeedback

Method of using sensory information to aid the control of involuntary physical processes, as in **Autogenic Training**, q.v. Typically, small electronic devices emitting sound or light signals are used to amplify the information available to the trainee. For example, if it is desired to achieve relaxation that will allow an improved blood flow to the hands and feet, a device monitoring electrical skin resistance is applied to the fingers and the trainee is instructed and encouraged to relax completely. As his peripheral blood supply changes so does the meter reading on the biofeedback device, allowing the trainee to register his success in relaxing and identify the physical sensations that led to success, as well as psychologically reinforcing him in his efforts. Ideally the trainee should eventually be able to dispense with the biofeedback device after it has served its purpose of helping to recognise his own physical state. For details of products and training in their use contact Audio Ltd, 26 Wendell Road, London W12. Tel: 081–743–1518. Knowledge of these techniques is a useful adjunct to a career in relaxation and stress reduction.

Bodywork

A term used to describe a range of physical approaches to health of mind and body. The assumption is usually that the state of the body mirrors the state of the mind and emotions, so that work on tensions and distortions in the body can help release the whole person for further growth. A sound massage training is a useful basis for most of these types of work.

Brainwave devices

These are electronic machines, usually portable, which can match by sound and/or light the rhythms of the brain at different frequencies, so as to reproduce Beta, Alpha, Theta and Delta rhythms which correspond to different states of mind. This technique is sometimes referred to as instant meditation. Benefits claimed include improved concentration and learning, deep relaxation, enhanced creativity and memory, improved sleep patterns. These, it is believed, can lead to stress and pain reduction, reduction of addictions and of depression and anxiety. Apart from the obvious relevance of these instruments to brain function research, there seem to be few career opportunities except in hiring out instruments in a commercial settings. NB: these devices should not be used by anyone who has epilepsy, high blood pressure or a heart condition or an electronic implant of any kind.

Chapman's reflexes

These are reflexes set up by contractions arising from neglected damage to internal organs. Often secondary trigger points will have arisen in apparently unrelated areas. An experienced naturopath or osteopath can remove the contraction, though if the pain pathways have been established for a long time the obliteration can also take time. This type of work should not be learned or practised on its own but as part of a proper naturopathic or osteopathic training. The properly trained practitioner will of course wish to remove his patient's discomfort but pain does not come without a reason and he will make it his business to get to the cause. This may involve long term treatment and advice or referral to other sources of help.

Chelation therapy

Chelation refers to the Greek word for clawing, specifically clawing away arterial plaque which narrows arteries and leads to heart disease and many associated problems. The two main ways in which this can be done are by nutritional means and by infusion of a solution of ethylene-diaminetetra-acetic acid. The first can be done with the help of a **Nutritional Adviser**, the second needs medically qualified personnel. Usually the two are used together as reputable clinics offering infusion also offer a maintenance programme for their patients. A sphere of employment for medical personnel and for nutritionists, usually working in cooperation.

Clinical ecology

Name given by doctors to a specialisation that traces health problems to pollution or other noxious influences in the environment. Clinical ecologists tend to focus upon allergic reactions, that is reactions mediated through the immune system, whereas naturopaths and other complementary practitioners tend to look more widely at the effects of food, water and environment on wellbeing. The profession has made only a limited impact, probably because specialists in the subject, in accordance with medical etiquette, accept referrals only via the patient's GP who may not believe in the idea at all. Also the National Health Service, which has to deal with many acute problems on a limited budget, understandably cannot give a high priority to funding posts for illnesses that are chronic, various and indefinite, consisting mainly of subjective reports of feelings of unwellness. **Naturopathy**, whose approach would be to remove the patient from a noxious environment while encouraging public measures to reduce pollution, stimulate his own vital powers and optimise his diet is probably the best hope for most sufferers. Those who wish to make a career in this field would probably contribute best by training in medicine and spreading the ideas of clinical ecology through general practice. An idea of the type of research involved and its popular application may be gained from: King, D.S. and Mandell, M., 'A double-blind study of allergic cerebro-vicscero-somatic malfunctions evoked by provocative sub-lingual challenge with allergen extracts', *Proceedings 12th Advanced Seminar in Clinical Ecology*, Key Biscayne, 1978 and Mackarness, R. *Not All In The Mind*, Pan Books, London, 1976.

Co-counselling

Technique whereby two people who both feel the need for counselling to overcome personal problems agree to act as counsellors for each other. They are trained in counselling methods and taught the rules by which each is client or counsellor by turns. Co-counselling usually takes place in participants' homes in two hour sessions – one hour for each partner to fill each role. During the sixties and seventies there were thriving European and American networks affiliated to Co-Counsellors International. Contact: John Heron, Assistant Director (Medical Education) British Postgraduate Medical Federation, 33 Millman Street, London WC1N 3EJ Tel: 071–831–6222. As the technique works on a mutual help basis, there is little possibility of developing a career in this technique except perhaps as a lecturer or organiser.

Colonic irrigation

Method of artificial bowel evacuation. As the name implies, it differs from the simple enema in sending the water higher up the colon. The theory is that many health problems may be caused by retained, impacted faecal material and that they can be relieved by washing this out and allowing the bowel to develop improved tone and better habits of evacuation. These ideas are not new and enjoy periods of popularity and relative neglect, often, apparently, depending on endorsement from public figures. For example, in a former age Sarah Bernhardt and Liane de Pougy were believed to owe their slimness, dazzling complexions and vivacity to their habits of bowel hygiene. Modern machines have eliminated many of the aesthetic disadvantages associated with the practice. Unfortunately they are expensive and this had led to methods of marketing machines and training as a package which may hinder acceptance in the British setting.

Cupping

Technique used until the early years of this century by the European medical profession. It involves introducing a wisp of lighted cotton into a small glass cup and inverting it on the skin. The heat and the vacuum thus created caused a blister and loss of blood. This procedure was known as dry cupping. Wet cupping involved the same procedure with the aggravation that the area was scarified with a lancet to promote the production of blood. As with the use of leeches, the aim was to reduce an underlying inflammation. Cupping was a standard treatment for such illnesses as pneumonia and pleurisy. It is sometimes confused with Oriental procedures such as *Moxibustion* which appear superficially similar but differ in their theory and effect.

Dianetics

System of de-programming human beings promulgated by the late L.Ron Hubbard, founder of the Church of

Scientology. In ideas and vocabulary it appears to draw on information theory, Ouspensky, depth psychology and psychoanalysis. Progress in Dianetics is mandatory for adherents of the Church of Scientology who pay for different levels of analysis and progress up the hierarchy until they reach the stages when they are judged competent to apply the system to their juniors. Following the death of L.Ron Hubbard, rival groups of followers have claimed to be the true heirs to the teachings, property and name of his organisation.

Eeman polarity screens

Devices invented by L.E. Eeman to enhance the body's own ability to heal itself by its own electromagnetic forces. Eeman's book *Co-operative Healing: the Curative Properties of Human Radiations* is out of print (Frederick Muller, 1947), but his polarity screens are available from Life Force, BCM, Box 8211, London WC1N 3XX. See also polarity therapy. Trials at Crystal Connection, 23 Camden Lock, London NW1 8AF.

Fasting See *Naturopathy*

Feldenkrais technique

Based on work of Moshe Feldenkrais, this technique aims to develop full function of the body by study and recapitulation of natural movements and breathing techniques through series of exercises. Claims improvement in back troubles and various musculoskeletal and neurological problems. Common in the United States of America, much less widespread in Britain, it has much in common with **Alexander Technique**. See Feldenkrais, M. 1972, *Awareness through Movement: Health exercises for personal growth*. Harper & Row, New York.

Floating

Technique developed following sensory deprivation experiments of Dr John Lilly. The subject is enclosed in a sound and light proof tank of saline solution concentrated enough to cause his body to float free. Benefits are alleged to include complete relaxation and harmonisation of the right

COMPLEMENTARY MEDICINE   163

and left side of the brain. Career possibilities concern the management of businesses providing these facilities for the public.

Gerson therapy

Dr Max Gerson (1881–1959) would have probably been surprised to find his work regarded as a part of complementary medicine. His view that most disease can be traced to habits of living and eating that damage the body's own healing powers and in particular the function of the liver is in the naturopathic tradition. Now his methods seem to be used mainly in cancer therapy. For an account see Beata Bishop, 1985, *A Time to Heal*, Severn House, London.

Group analytic therapy

Type of psychotherapy developed by S.H. Foulkes, in which the therapeutic process takes place in and among a group of patients. Both medical personnel and lay psychotherapists work in this speciality. Training is by undergoing analysis and attending seminars and workshops over a period of several years. Contact: Group Analytic Society, (London), 1 Daleham Gardens, London NW3. Tel: 071–431–2693. Book: S.H. Foulkes and E.J. Anthony, *Group Psychotherapy*, Pelican, London, 1957.

Hair analysis

Technique used for diagnostic purposes. The theory is that traces of minerals and some other chemicals absorbed by human beings from their food or environment can be found in their hair. A snippet of hair from a patient is sent to a laboratory, where it is washed so that the contaminants are extracted in solution. The resulting solution is analysed spectrographically and a report sent back. Dietary or clinical ecology advice may be given on the basis of the report. Obviously the usefulness of the technique depends very much on the interpretation of the results and here it is possible to go badly wrong if too little is known about the patient's circumstances. A well known historical example is the allegation that Napoleon was poisoned by persons unknown with arsenic, based on the discovery of traces in preserved locks of his hair. In fact the cause of his death seems to have been stomach cancer and the arsenic in his hair was traced to the fashionable green paint on the walls of his bedroom. Hair analysis can be used as a diagnostic tool by many different types of practitioner, especially if they suspect an environmental cause of their patient's symptoms. Care but no special skill is needed on the part of the practitioner. His contribution is his conscientious investigation of the background. The people who actually carry out the test are laboratory staff. They need the usual training in chemical analysis, based on science A levels and science degrees.

Heilpraktiker
German naturopathic profession. Practitioners are trained in a range of natural therapies and are more like general practitioners than the specialist practitioners in this country, though most of them have a preferred skill. They are licensed to practise after they have completed their training by coming before a board of doctors and proving that they can identify conditions that should be referred elsewhere. There are reports that these medical boards are now refusing to pass successful candidates and this is believed to herald a campaign to abolish the status of the heilpraktikers.

Hydrotherapy
The Austrian Pastor Kneipp brought together his own experience and much existing folklore on the use of bathing and water as a means to preserve health. Many of the practices he suggests have the effect of stimulating circulation, promoting elimination and cleansing through skin or bowels and toning the muscles. Today they are generally taught as part of **Naturopathy**. Kneipp's own work is reprinted from time to time and can still be bought in English as *My Water Cure* in many different editions.

Iridology
This diagnostic technique is based on the idea that the iris of the eye reflects the state of the body of which it is part. Detailed maps have been developed of the textures and patterns relating to different health problems. The main tools of the iridologist are a magnifying lens to study the iris

and a camera to record its changes. Many accounts have been written to record its changes. Many accounts have been written of changes monitored during the return of patients to their normal health. Most people would find it credible that the more delicate tissues of the body would register changes in the health of the whole. Less credible, perhaps, are later suggestions that emotional tendencies towards, for example, suicide or incest can be detected from the study of the iris.

A distance learning course in Iridology is available from the National Council and Register of Iridology, 40 Stokewood Road, Swinton, Bournemouth BH3 7NC. Secretary: Sheelagh Colton. A diploma is awarded on the results of the final examination. Iridology alone is unlikely to provide a livelihood, but can be useful to back up other skills and to confirm diagnoses obtained by other means.

Kirlian photography
A system of high energy photography that appears to record the level of vitality of living things. For details of its use in health studies contact: R. Steel, 173 Woburn Towers, Northolt UB5 6HU. Tel: 081–841–3458.

Light treatment for the eyes
Coloured light in an appropriate range has been found to benefit many different types of eye problem. For information contact: Mrs Mary Simpkins, 7 Old Orchard Road, Eastbourne, Sussex BN21 1DB   Tel: 0323–331703

Macrobiotics
System of diet propounded by a Japanese, George Ohsawa, after World War II. It attempts to achieve a balance of yin and yang to promote harmony of the whole person leading to total health. Details and training in cooking and dietetics from East West Centre, 108 Old Street, London.

Magnetic therapy
This description has been given at different times to a whole range of therapies based on various of the electro-magnetic properties of the human body. It would be impossible to describe all the variations but a selection follows. **1**   It has

been observed that fractured bones knit more quickly in frosty weather and that the same effect can be produced in summer by putting the injured part in a magnetic field. Similar results are claimed for other types of injury but doubts have been raised about the wisdom of speeding up the normal rate of cell activity. **2**   Techniques have been developed in Japan of applying small magnets to the acupuncture points with the aim of enhancing the healing process, particularly for problems usually dealt with by osteopathic means.

Magnetism
Confusion has arisen from the use in France and some other European countries of the expression magnetism to refer to the activities of healers. This usage is a legacy from the time of Anton Mesmer who attributed his success in what seems to have been a form of hypnotherapy to his control of magnetic fluid in his patients.

Medical palmistry
Has attracted ridicule for the idea that the lines in the hand can be used to foretell susceptibility to disease or can record events in the client's medical history. However, before the genetic basis of Down's syndrome was understood, the typical formation of the palm was one of the most easily read signs of what was then called mongolism.

Megavitamin Psychiatry See **Orthomolecular Psychiatry**

Metamorphic technique
A technique developed by Robert St John and based on ideas found in Emmanuel Swedenborg's *Doctrine of Correspondences*. The basic idea is that the human embryo goes through a number of stages during its development and that many types of mental and physical handicap result from imperfect completion of each stage. St John taught that energies blocked at these stages can be released by working on the spinal reflexes in the hands, feet and head, setting free healing processes of body, mind and spirit. Many parents of handicapped children have found the

Technique helpful and it is mainly in the disabled community that any career opportunities are to be found. Contact: Metamorphic Association, 67 Ritherden Road, London SW17 8QE Tel: 081–672–5951. Book: Gaston Saint-Pierre & Debbie Shapiro, *The Metamorphic Technique, Principles and Practice*. Element Books, ISBN 1–85230–032–9.

Moxibustion
Burning of moxa, a preparation of wormwood, on acupuncture points to stimulate a desired reaction. See **Acupuncture** and **Chinese Medicine**.

Myotherapy, Bonnie Prudden Certified
Name patented by US citizen Bonnie Prudden for a technique of releasing trigger points caused by insults to muscles. Bonnie Prudden achieved fame for helping President Kennedy's back problems. The technique she uses is one that is well understood by many doctors and complementary practitioners. Equivalent treatment is taught to **Osteopaths** and Sports **Massage** practitioners. These trainings are therefore a more sensible basis for a career. NB: Pressure may be used to a painful degree.

Neuro-linguistic programming
Name given to extensions of Ericksonian techniques of hypnotherapy developed by Bandler and Grinder in the United States of America While they rightly stress the importance of the information that can be obtained from observing the client's preferred mode of interaction and can be very effective when correctly used they do not replace sound classical technique based on an understanding of the psychology of the patient's situation.

Neuro-muscular technique
A very gentle method of manipulating soft tissues, especially appropriate to the elderly or frail and in cases where there is structural damage. This skill is part of the armoury of an osteopath.

Nutritional eye health care
Experience of 40 years' work in Africa where much

blindness is caused early in life by malnutrition led Stanley
Evans to see whether he could help sufferers in Britain by
improving their absorption of essential nutrients. The
following titles give an idea of the range of possibilities.
Evans, Stanley C., *Effect of Alcohol and Tobacco on Eye Health*
£4.25; *Help for Cataract Sufferers*, £4.25; *Help for Glaucoma
Sufferers*, £6.00; *Help for Progressive Myopes*, £4.25; *Help for
Squint Sufferers*, £4.25; *Prevention of Blindness in Britain*,
£4.25; *Wholefood for Beginners*, £4.25. For books and training
contact Teecoll Optical Products Limited, Sanctuary House,
Oulton Road, Lowestoft, Suffolk NR32 4QZ Tel: 0502–
583294.

Ortho-molecular medicine/psychiatry
The term is used by those who stress the effect of nutrition
or of external environmental factors on the physical and
mental health of human beings and of growing children
especially. They look in particular at the effects at cellular
level and at the molecular input of cellular nutrition. Career
involvement is probably best via a training in **Nutrition** for
complementary practitioners and via training in **Clinical
Ecology** for doctors. Controversy about the subject has been
reactivated recently by studies of the effects of Vitamin
supplements on the tested I.Q.s of Welsh school children.
No doubt research and counter-research will be produced.
The practical difficulties of providing definitive evidence are
aggravated by what many feel to be political implications of
findings on either side. A flavour of the work in the field and
the issues involved may be gathered from: Fogel, M.L. Auto-
fumes may Lower your Kids I.Q., *Psychology Today*, 13(8):
108, January, 1980; Schauss, A., *Diet, Crime and Delinquency*,
Parker House, Berkeley, California, 1980; Watson, G.,
Nutrition and your Mind, Harper and Row, New York, 1972.

Primal therapy
Based on the work of Dr Arthur Janov, attempts to help
patients overcome their problems by re-living earliest
memories of overwhelming experiences, notably birth.
Contact: London Association of Primal Therapy, 18a
Laurier Road, London NW5 1SH Tel: 071–267–9616.

COMPLEMENTARY MEDICINE   169

Propolis

This is a substance produced by bees to seal apertures in their hives. Apiarists were the first to discover the anti-bacterial and healing properties of propolis. As only small quantities are produced during any one season its price is high and for some bee-keepers it is a highly profitable sideline to their honey business. It seems to be used mostly for self-medication by people who buy it direct from apiaries and has a good word of mouth reputation for relieving rheumatic conditions, healing small wounds and sore throats. There may be commercial opportunities for people who are already in bee-farming or pharmaceuticals, but the problems of supply, standardisation and shelf-life have so far proved insuperable.

Psionic medicine

This term is usually used to describe their work by doctors doing what is usually described by others as radionics. There is a Psionic Medical Society open only to doctors and dentists. Its members are denoted by the letters F (Fellow) or M (Member) IPM. Contact: Psionic Medical Society, Garden Cottage, Beacon Hill Park, Hindhead, Surrey.

Psychic Surgery

The term refers to two different main subjects: **1** There is a tradition in the Philippines and in some parts of South America of local healers performing operations that cause a miraculous cure. The patients are prepared by the healer's assistants and laid on an operating table. The healer, after suitable preparations which may include putting the patient into a light hypnotic trance, appears to make an incision, remove blood and other material which is thrown in a bucket and close the wound. A remarkable number of patients report relief of symptoms and appear to survive in reasonable health. However investigators have managed to secrete specimens of the blood and tissue which proved to come from chicken carcasses. Argument centres on whether any success is due to skilled choice of patients who have hysterical symptoms or to the placebo effect. In the latter case, the effect would presumably be enhanced by the impressive trappings of modern medical procedures in countries where these are not easily available. In Britain this would not apply and anyone who set up to provide psychic surgery of this kind would be likely to be suspected as a fraudulent conjurer. **2** A healer, George Chapman, found himself in touch with a spirit whom he identified as William Lang, an ophthalmic surgeon who had lived in the latter half of the nineteenth century. Chapman saw himself as the channel for Lang's work of healing which continued his earthly surgical work on a psychic level.

Psychodrama

A form of group psychotherapy developed in the work of Jacob Moreno (born 1892). He realised that powerful effects could come from actually doing mental and emotional acts rather than merely talking about them. Accordingly the patient upon whom the group is temporarily focused will be asked to be himself in the situations that he describes and other group members will play to him other characters in the drama of his life. This method is seldom used in its pure form today, but has been influential in **Dramatherapy** and in a variety of approaches to personal development such as assertiveness training.

Psychosynthesis

A system of psychotherapy developed by Roberto Assagioli. Among psychotherapists he seems to have been remarkable for his absence of dogma and his refusal to force his patients into a fixed idea of what they should be like. For an introduction to the ideas, read Assagioli, Roberto, *The Act of Will*, Penguin. Contact for treatments and training: Institute of Psychosynthesis, Highwood Park, Nan Clarke's Lane, Mill Hill, London NW7 Tel: 081–959–3372.

Pulsed electro-magnetic emissions (PEME)

A type of electro-magnetic therapy reputed to be particularly useful in speeding healing of both fractures and damage to soft tissue. The equipment was developed and is now most notably used by an osteopath. It is unlikely to be possible for anyone without this level of training to be able to use it successfully. The machine is heavy so that patients need to come to the centre where it is used rather than having it transported to them. Does not provide a career in itself, but should be seen as a supplement or development for osteopaths, chiropractors and orthopaedic specialists. For training and equipment supply contact Blue Stone Clinic, 114 Upper Harley Street, London NW1 5HE   Tel: 071–935–7933.

Pulsing

A style of **Massage** that uses rhythms in tune with those of the body to release tensions that have been inhibiting physical and emotional development. Inspired by the ideas of Wilhelm Reich. To get the best from a study of pulsing a sound basic knowledge of **Massage** and anatomy is needed.

Radiance technique

Another name for Reiki, a form of healing, started in the United States of America supposedly with Japanese inspiration.

Radiesthesia

This word is sometimes used as an equivalent for radionics and denotes the sort of perceptions supposed to be at work in dowsing and other forms of healing and divining. Radiesthesia is a term transliterated from the French and is generally preferred by doctors working in this field. It is therefore useful as an indicator of the general orientation of the speaker.

Radionics

Originated in the nineteenth century with the work of Dr Abrams, Director of Studies at Stanford University Medical School. Viewing man as a totality, it directs healing energies by means of various instruments at the subtle etheric, spiritual and mental bodies of the patient. Abrams and his successors originated the idea that different diseases had different rates, a numerical value corresponding to characteristic frequencies. Practitioners are currently divided as to the amount of training needed and the efficacy of different types of instrument. The Keys College of Radionics, Sycamore Farm, Chadlington, Oxford offers training leading to membership of the Radionic Register.

For an account of the current state of the art read L. Dower's *Radionics*, Thorsons.

Rational emotive psychotherapy

An approach that involves both the emotions and the cognitive faculties of the mind on the basis that neither can function fully without the other. By no means a soft option, it is particularly favoured in treatment of those whose behaviour has resulted in damage to others. For example, dangerous drivers or sexual offenders typically maintain that their actions are perfectly reasonable and that any damage is the fault of their victims. They are unlikely to change until they have fully understood its impact on other people and that those people are as real as themselves. The same approach can help many disturbed and unhappy people. Details of training available from the Centre for Stress Management, 156 Westcombe Hill, London SE3 7DH Tel: 081–293–4114.

Regression therapy

In the early days of psychoanalysis, when all psychic problems were attributed to repressed childhood trauma or fantasies, it was customary to take patients back, either by ordinary memory or in a hypnotic state, to the time of the supposed experience. Some psychoanalysts found that their patients went back before birth and recounted experiences supposed to have happened while they were in the womb. From this it was a short step to the discovery of people who seemed able to go even further back to past lives. This is now the significance in which the word regression is generally used. Preparation for this type of work is via a sound training in **Hypnotherapy** and **Psychotherapy**.

Reichian therapy

Wilhelm Reich died in prison (1957) in the United States of America because his desire to develop a physics of psychological forces led him to offer treatments and machines that seemed to his medical contemporaries to be fraudulent. His two key concepts of bioenergy and armouring (that musculature records emotional experience and defends the individual against emotional shocks) have been widely influential and may be traced in many different types of psychotherapy and bodywork.

Soul directed therapy

Cooperation between a medium and a psychiatrist in which the insights of both are used to assess the patient's spiritual and emotional state and help with problems and future directions. Planning a career in the field obviously depends upon a number of imponderables such as chancing to find the right partnership of skills. It would be difficult for anyone with both skills to play both parts to the full, though this is not inconceivable. The best guidance about the possibilities would probably be obtained by consulting the current leading practitioners of the subject. Inge Hooper and Lisa Sands, 22 Caesar Court, Basinghall Gardens, Sutton, Surrey SM2 6AR   Tel: 081–643–4255.

T'ai Chi Chu'an

A Martial Art and system of exercise sometimes referred to as Chinese shadow boxing. The smooth and gentle movements are a form of meditation in action. Physical benefits include increased suppleness and strength, with decreased risk of cardiovascular disease, brittle bones and

age-associated deformities. Emotional effects reported
include improved mood, reduction in tension, depression
and tiredness. The methods generally used in the West are
the long and short form of the Yang style, named after Yang
Lu-chan who lived in Peking in the nineteenth century.
Contact: The British T'ai Chi Chu'an Association, 7 Upper
Wimpole Street, London W1M 7TD.

Therapeutic touch

Term invented by American nurse, Dolores Krieger for a
systematic method of hand healing. The name has
sometimes caused confusion by suggesting a form of
massage, but the patient's physical body is not in fact
touched. The nurse gathers herself into a meditative state
and then rebalances the patient's energies by moving her
hands over the energy fields of the body. Colour meditation
is simultaneously used to enhance the effect. Krieger was
Professor of Nursing at New York University and was able
to prove her success in a number of clinical investigations.
Therapeutic touch is now an accepted part of nursing
technique taught in nursing schools in Canada and the
United States of America. Krieger, D., *The Therapeutic Touch:
How to Use Your Hands to Help and Heal*, Englewood Cliffs,
New Jersey, Prentice Hall, 1979.

Tissue salts

Dr Schuessler was the inventor of a series of nine tissue salts
each of which is appropriate for a particular group of
illnesses which are regarded as evidences of deficiency of the
particular substances. The salts are home remedies for the
medicine cabinet rather than the basis of an independent
career.

Toning

The modern name for a practice that has roots deep in
many primitive cultures of tuning in to a tone that is
therapeutically appropriate for a patient and producing it as
a powerful humming or booming sound. The chanting of
shamans or medicine men usually incorporate sound of this
kind. Throat sounds producing a growling sound that can
have a hypnotic effect form part of the religious practices of

Tibetan monks and it has been suggested that the alpenhorn of Switzerland has its origin in ancient shamanic rites.

Touch for health

Movement for home use of the teachings of **Applied Kinesiology**. Non-professionals are taught basic techniques which can be used for self-help or mild family problems. It should not be regarded as a licence to practise professionally. The training courses are not therefore the basis of a professional career. British Contact: Adrian Voce, 8 Railey Mews, Kentish Town, London NW5 2PA Tel: 071–482–0698. The British Touch for Health Association, 29 Bushey Close, High Wycombe, Bucks HP12 3HL   Tel: 0494–37409

Tragerwork

A system of bodywork developed by Milton Trager, who specialised in rehabilitation of polio victims. It is particularly relaxing, gentle and playful, featuring rocking and a number of mental exercises referred to as Mentastics. So far it is not widely known or used in Britain and some writers question whether the system itself or Trager's healing personality was more important in his success.

Transformational Therapy Another name for *Regression Therapy*. q.v.

Unani-tibb

System of medicine prevalent in Pakistan. It is now considered to be thoroughly Islamic but its roots seem to lie with the Ancient Greek tradition received via Persia and with the **Ayurvedic** system of Ancient India. The Hamdard Institute of Karachi is pursuing a project of research into the usefulness of this system of medicine and of traditional medicinal plants. The results are published in their Journal.

Urine therapy

Interest revives from time to time in the theory that the urine contains many minerals beneficial to the person who has excreted it. In India there persists a small following for this theory and rumours that individual politicians owe their

health and longevity to this therapy have been influential in
Indian political life. It is unlikely to form the basis for a
career in Britain. Support for the practice may be found in:
Armstrong, J.W., 1964, *Water of Life*, C.W. Daniel, Saffron
Walden, Essex.

Zone therapy

Name sometimes used as equivalent to **Reflexology**. During
the nineteenth century Austrian and American doctors in
particular discovered a vertical division of the body into
zones with reflexes related to points within the same zone,
closely resembling the patterns familiar in Chinese
Acupuncture. They developed the use of these points
particularly for pain control, but their work was overtaken
by the discovery of anaesthetics which removed public
interest in other types of analgesia. Modern **Reflexology** is a
specialised development of this work.

The Institute for Complementary Medicine

For specific career advice, for application forms for any
division of the British Register of Complementary
Practitioners and for referrals, please write to the Institute
for Complementary Medicine, Unit 4, Tavern Quay, Rope
Street, Rotherhithe, London SE16, stating your needs as
clearly as possible and enclosing a large, stamped, addressed
envelope. Gifts of stamps to help defray the costs of
stationery and reproduction would be much appreciated.